Integrating Instruction

in

Science

Strategies, Activities, Projects, Tools, and Techniques

by Imogene Forte and Sandra Schurr

Incentive Publications, Inc.
Nashville, Tennessee

Illustrated by Marta Drayton
Cover by Geoffrey Brittingham
Edited by Jan Keeling

ISBN 0-86530-321-5

PRINTED IN THE UNITED STATES OF AMERICA

TABLE OF CONTENTS

Using Integrated Instructional Strategies to Accommodate Differing Learning Styles, Abilities, and Interests

Using Multiple Intelligences as an Instructional Tool

Using Learning Stations as an Instructional Tool

Using the Read and Relate Concept as an Instructional Tool

Using Integrated Instructional Strategies to Develop Problem-solving and Higher-order Thinking Skills

Using Bloom's Taxonomy as an Instructional Tool

Using Williams' Taxonomy as an Instructional Tool

Using Investigation Cards as an Instructional Tool

Using Calendars as an Instructional Tool

Using Integrated Instructional Strategies to Promote Cooperative Learning and Group Interaction

Using Integrated Instructional Strategies to Facilitate Authentic Assessment

A Very Practical Appendix

Preface

Middle grades educators are meeting the challenges of student-centered education with new teaching methods that help create a positive learning climate. Middle grades science educators want to know how to use these new instructional strategies and organizational procedures in ways that are specifically designed for the science classroom.

Integrating Instruction in Science was created for science educators at the middle grade level. The high-interest activities, many of which highlight conservation and preservation, cover topics in the major areas of science, including the following:

- Astronomy
- Biology
- Botany
- Chemistry
- Ecology
- Geology
- Medicine
- Meteorology
- Physics
- Zoology

In each of five major sections you will find a comprehensive overview of a particular instructional focus accompanied by exciting activities that are meant to be used as well as to serve as examples.

USING INTEGRATED INSTRUCTIONAL STRATEGIES TO ACCOMMODATE DIFFERING LEARNING STYLES, ABILITIES, AND INTERESTS features guidelines for incorporating the Multiple Intelligences, Learning Stations, and Read and Relate tasks into the preparation of high-quality lesson plans and student assignments.

USING INTEGRATED INSTRUCTIONAL STRATEGIES TO DEVELOP PROBLEM-SOLVING AND HIGHER-ORDER THINKING SKILLS offers guidelines for infusing higher-order thinking skills into the educational process through the use of cognitive taxonomies, self-directed investigation cards, and calendars. The cognitive taxonomies offer great foundations for the design of interdisciplinary units, student worksheets, learning stations, and group projects.

USING INSTRUCTIONAL STRATEGIES TO PROMOTE COOPERATIVE LEARNING AND GROUP INTERACTION presents valuable collaborative processes such as Think/Pair/Share, Three-Step Interview, Circle of Knowledge, Team Learning, Round Table, and Jigsaw.

USING INTEGRATED INSTRUCTIONAL STRATEGIES TO FACILITATE AUTHENTIC ASSESSMENT shows how to effectively implement product, performance, and portfolio assessment practices. Included is a complete sample portfolio based on an interdisciplinary unit on the Solar System.

Finally, **A VERY PRACTICAL APPENDIX** provides high-interest strategies and activities to integrate social studies, math, and language arts into the science curriculum; topics for student reports and journal writing; a research outline and blank planning outlines to help in the creation of original lesson plans; and an annotated bibliography. A comprehensive index is invaluable in keeping this wealth of information at your fingertips.

In short, this book is a must for all science educators, for those on interdisciplinary teams as well as those in self-contained classrooms. It offers a collection of instructional strategies that were designed for heterogeneous groups of students in an educational setting that will allow every student to be successful. It clarifies theoretical principles and offers activities that cover a wide range of important science topics. Best of all, its content is fresh, original, and of interest to contemporary middle grades students.

Using Integrated Instructional Strategies to Accommodate Differing Learning Styles, Abilities, and Interests

Using Multiple Intelligences as an Instructional Tool

Howard Gardner's Theory of the Multiple Intelligences provides teachers with an excellent model for the design of interdisciplinary units, student worksheets, learning stations, and group projects. Gardner is quick to point out that (1) every student has at least one dominant intelligence (although he or she may have more than one); (2) these intelligences can all be nurtured, strengthened, and taught over time; (3) the intelligences do not exist in isolation but interface and interact with one another when completing a task; and (4) the intelligences provide teachers with seven different ways to approach the curriculum. Gardner has identified and described seven major intelligences:

VERBAL/LINGUISTIC DOMINANCE
Students strong in this type of intelligence have highly developed verbal skills, and often think in words. They do well on written assignments, enjoy reading, and are good at communicating and expressing themselves.

LOGICAL/MATHEMATICAL DOMINANCE
Students strong in this intelligence think in abstractions and handle complex concepts, and they readily see patterns or relationships in ideas. They like to work with numbers and perform mathematical operations, and approach problem-solving exercises with logic and rational thought.

VISUAL/SPATIAL DOMINANCE
Students think in images, symbols, colors, pictures, patterns, and shapes. They like to perform tasks that require "seeing with the mind's eye"—tasks that require them to visualize, imagine, pretend, or form images.

BODY/KINESTHETIC DOMINANCE
Students dominant in this intelligence have a strong body awareness and a sharp sense of physical movement. They communicate best through body language, physical gestures, hands-on activities, active demonstrations, and performance tasks.

MUSICAL/RHYTHMIC DOMINANCE
Students with this dominant intelligence enjoy music, rhythmic patterns, variations in tones or rhythms, and sounds. They enjoy listening to music, composing music, interpreting music, performing to music, and learning with music playing in the background.

INTERPERSONAL DOMINANCE

Students with this dominant intelligence thrive on person-to interactions and team activities. They are sensitive to the feelings and needs of others and are skilled team members, discussion leaders, and peer mediators.

INTRAPERSONAL DOMINANCE

Students with this dominant intelligence prefer to work alone because they are self-reflective, self-motivated, and in tune with their own feelings, beliefs, strengths, and thought processes. They respond to intrinsic rather than extrinsic rewards and may demonstrate great wisdom and insight when presented with personal challenges and independent-study opportunities.

The Theory of Multiple Intelligences can be used as a guide for the teacher who is interested in creating lesson plans that address one or more of the intelligences on a daily basis. Teachers should ask themselves the following questions when attempting to develop or evaluate classroom activities using seven intelligences:

(1) What tasks require students to write, speak, or read?

(2) What tasks require students to engage in problem solving, logical thought, or calculations?

(3) What tasks require students to create images or visual aids and to analyze colors, textures, forms, or shapes?

(4) What tasks require students to employ body motions, manipulations, or hands-on approaches to learning?

(5) What tasks require students to incorporate music, rhythm, pitch, tones, or environmental sounds in their work?

(6) What tasks require students to work in groups and to interact with others?

(7) What tasks require students to express personal feelings, insights, beliefs, and self-disclosing ideas?

The following pages provide the teacher with several examples of how the Multiple Intelligences have been used as an organizing structure when designing classroom materials and assignments.

Rocks and Minerals
A Rocky Start

VERBAL /LINGUISTIC
Make a dictionary of 20 "rock words" whose meanings you have learned. Illustrate your dictionary.

LOGICAL /MATHEMATICAL
Pretend you are a geologist who is being interviewed for a newspaper article. Explain to the reporter how one can distinguish an igneous rock from a sedimentary rock, and how one can distinguish both from a metamorphic rock.

VISUAL /SPATIAL
Draw an outline of a United States map and mark the locations where five to ten different kinds of rocks or minerals can be found. Label these locations.

BODY/KINESTHETIC
Design ten different "rocks and minerals" trivia cards.

MUSICAL /RHYTHMIC
Select a favorite "rock and roll" song. Use it as background music for a silent filmstrip on rocks and minerals. To create the filmstrip, draw your filmstrip sections on a piece of adding machine tape or a roll of shelf paper and construct a filmstrip viewer from a cardboard box.

INTERPERSONAL
Work with a friend to research the history behind some unusual rocks or rock formations that have become historical landmarks and/or tourist attractions. Design a fold-out presentation to share your findings.

INTRAPERSONAL
Determine whether you would rather be a geologist or a gemologist. What are your reasons?

Weather/Climate

Weather or Not

VERBAL/LINGUISTIC
Read several myths or legends in which weather plays a significant role, and then write an original myth of your own using real weather terms, concepts, and conditions in the telling of your story.

LOGICAL/MATHEMATICAL
Define and describe the weather elements that determine the climate of a given location.

VISUAL/SPATIAL
Create a weather montage (or collage) that shows as many concepts and elements involved in our study of climate as you can find. Write a one-page summary or explanation of the montage and paste it on the back side of the project.

BODY/KINESTHETIC
Every day for one week, cut out the weather map found in your local newspaper. Use the maps to prepare a short television talk show entitled: "Our Weather Week in Review."

MUSICAL/RHYTHMIC
Do some research to learn about Indian rain dances, and then create an original dance routine of your own.

INTERPERSONAL
Stage a debate between the two seasons Winter and Summer, with an emphasis on the elements of weather and climate.

INTRAPERSONAL
Write a short essay describing how you feel about the climate of the area where you live.

Laws of Motion

Forces in Action

VERBAL/LINGUISTIC
Create a simple glossary to define these important terms related to Newton's Laws of Motion: velocity, acceleration, motion, inertia, friction, mass, gravity, force, and weight.

LOGICAL/MATHEMATICAL
Briefly state and give an example of the Laws of Motion (known as Newton's Laws, named after Sir Isaac Newton).

VISUAL/SPATIAL
Create a set of diagrams to demonstrate your understanding of the three Laws of Motion.

BODY/KINESTHETIC
Act out a series of events to demonstrate your understanding of Newton's Laws.

MUSICAL/RHYTHMIC
Select a piece of classical music that seems to reflect and demonstrate the actions and interactions of Newton's Laws of Motion.

INTERPERSONAL
Working with other members of your class, create a handbook that illustrates Newton's First, Second, and Third Laws of Motion. Your handbook should include illustrations, photographs, and written descriptions of examples of the laws that you observe in your everyday world.

INTRAPERSONAL
Collect a variety of simple moving toys such as a slinky, a yo-yo, a spinning top, a paper glider, and a hula hoop. Describe the motion of each toy when in use, the kind of force that makes the toy move, and how the motion of the toy could be changed. Select one of the toys that is most like you and write a paragraph explaining why.

Forms of Energy

Kinetic and Potential Energy

 ## VERBAL/LINGUISTIC
Write one good paragraph to describe the relationships between work, kinetic energy, and potential energy.

 ## LOGICAL/MATHEMATICAL
Conduct an experiment that demonstrates your understanding of ways to convert potential energy to kinetic energy.

 ## VISUAL/SPATIAL
Create a poster that shows how the transfer of energy can be compared to the transfer of money among people.

 ## BODY/KINESTHETIC
Make up a physical routine or dance to demonstrate different ways to convert potential energy to kinetic energy.

 ## MUSICAL/RHYTHMIC
Record sounds from the environment that seem to represent the conversion of energy forms. See if classmates can guess what is making or causing each sound.

 ## INTERPERSONAL
With a small group of peers, design a display or exhibit that teaches others about the concepts of potential and kinetic forms of energy.

 ## INTRAPERSONAL
In a short essay, determine the reasons you are more like potential energy or kinetic energy. Give many personal examples to support your position.

Table of the Elements

Secrets of the Periodic Table

VERBAL/LINGUISTIC
In your own words, describe the historical development and the current organization of the elements found on the periodic table.

LOGICAL/MATHEMATICAL
Brainstorm a list of properties, other than mass, that could be used to organize the elements of the periodic table. Use one of these properties to construct a new version of the existing periodic table.

VISUAL/SPATIAL
Copy each square of the existing periodic table on a 3" x 5" file card. Classify these cards in some meaningful way and write a paragraph explaining the rationale for your classification system.

BODY/KINESTHETIC
Draw diagrams demonstrating different bonding patterns and then orchestrate a dance showing several different bonding patterns.

MUSICAL/RHYTHMIC
Develop a rhythmic pattern of sounds to represent any ten elements of the periodic table. Teach your pattern of sounds to some peers and have them use it to represent the other elements of the periodic table.

INTERPERSONAL
Work with other members of the class to create a king-sized version of the periodic table for the bulletin board. Ask each student to select two elements from the periodic table and to use a square piece of paper to record the following information for each of the elements: symbol of the element, atomic mass, atomic number, and three interesting facts about the element itself.

INTRAPERSONAL
Express your personal opinion of the current organization of the periodic table. Does it make sense to you? Or would you have organized it differently had you been directing its development?

Biology/Medicine

Diseases

VERBAL/LINGUISTIC

Prepare a short but informative report on any five of the most common communicable childhood diseases in the United States.

LOGICAL/MATHEMATICAL

Determine the role of each of the following in the spread and/or prevention of childhood communicable diseases: antibodies, vaccines, viruses, bacteria, and parasites.

VISUAL/SPATIAL

Develop a board game about the body's immune system where the object of the game is to identify and destroy those substances that invade the body and cause a wide variety of diseases and illnesses.

BODY/KINESTHETIC

Write and perform a short play to promote good health practices for preventing common communicable diseases.

MUSICAL /RHYTHMIC

Compose a short lyrical poem, song, or jingle that captures a variety of sounds to represent various childhood illnesses and diseases.

INTERPERSONAL

Interview the immune system as if it were a guest on a talk show. Work with a partner to develop a set of interview questions and conduct the interview with one playing the role of the interviewer and the other of the interviewee.

INTRAPERSONAL

Maintain a health journal for a week in which you keep a record of both your healthy and unhealthy practices. Draw some "healthy" conclusions from your data about your personal life style.

Electricity
Electrical Connections

VERBAL/LINGUISTIC
Discuss "connections" between electricity and each of these concepts: lightning, electric eel, flashlight battery. Write your ideas in a short report.

LOGICAL/MATHEMATICAL
Create a series of math word problems to demonstrate the use of each of the following for measuring electricity. Remember that the current, or flow, of electricity is measured in amperes (amps); the force that pushes electrons through an electrical circuit is measured in volts; the resistance a material puts against the flow of electricity is measured in ohms; and the power of an electrical machine is measured in watts.

> **watts = voltage (volts) × current (amps)**
> **force (in volts) = current (in amperes) × resistance (in ohms)**
> **current (in amperes) = force (in volts) ÷ resistance (in ohms)**
> **resistance (in ohms) = force (volts) ÷ current (in amperes)**

VISUAL/SPATIAL
Construct a chart that shows materials that are conductors of electricity and materials that are not conductors of electricity.

BODY/KINESTHETIC
Draw a set of scenarios to show examples of static electricity in everyday situations.

MUSICAL/RHYTHMIC
Analyze the lyrics of the song "Opposites Attract" by Paula Abdul and relate them to what you know about electrical charges.

INTERPERSONAL
Batteries contain mercury, which is considered a hazardous waste when discarded in the environment. In fact, the small batteries found in watches, hearing aids, and cameras make up 25 percent of the hazardous wastes from households in the United States. Organize a panel to discuss the impact of batteries on the environment and the idea of mandatory recycling of them and/or of mandating that the manufacturers of batteries give consumers a surcharge when they return used batteries to the seller.

INTRAPERSONAL
What kind of situation in a person's life do you think can have a lot of "voltage"?

Zoology/Communications

Animal Talk

VERBAL/LINGUISTIC
Write a short essay with this topic sentence: "Each species of animal has its own way of communicating."

LOGICAL/MATHEMATICAL
Compare and contrast any five animals in terms of their methods of communication. Consider the sounds they make, the behaviors they exhibit, and the methods they use to protect themselves and to stake out their territory.

VISUAL/SPATIAL
Draw a series of animals in different habitats and show their methods of communication.

BODY/KINESTHETIC
Organize and play a game of charades showing various animal behaviors for communicating with one another.

MUSICAL/RHYTHMIC
Browse through a series of poetry books and locate at least five different poems that typify animal communication behaviors. Tape the reading of these poems to a background of appropriate musical selections.

INTERPERSONAL
Work with a group of peers to create a classroom mural whose theme is: "Talk to the Animals."

INTRAPERSONAL
Determine which animal species is most like you and give reasons for your choice.

Environmental Studies

Pollution

VERBAL/LINGUISTIC
Write a descriptive paragraph about each of the following types of pollution, defining and outlining the causes of each one: water pollution, air pollution, noise pollution, and land pollution.

LOGICAL/MATHEMATICAL
Construct a chart to compare and contrast water pollution, air pollution, noise pollution, and land pollution.

VISUAL/SPATIAL
Compile a scrapbook containing a wide variety of newspaper and magazine articles as well as pictures and photographs on the topic of pollution. Include captions and labels where appropriate. Write an introduction and a conclusion for your scrapbook.

BODY/KINESTHETIC
Role play the ways in which different citizen groups might react to or deal with various problems involving pollution.

MUSICAL/RHYTHMIC
Make an audiotape of environmental sounds that could be considered sound pollutants.

INTERPERSONAL
Work with a partner to determine the best response to this question: "How important is it to achieve consensus on a proposed plan of action for dealing with the problems of pollution?"

INTRAPERSONAL
Determine whether you agree or disagree with this statement recently made by a group of respected environmentalists: "Light pollution is rapidly becoming a problem in many major cities and towns, obscuring the night sky for many citizens." Give reasons for your feelings, observations, and/or opinions.

Scientists

Scientists of Our Living World

VERBAL/LINGUISTIC

There are several different types of scientists who study the world of living things. Read to learn what each of the following scientists is most likely to study: Botanist, Zoologist, Microbiologist, Cytologist, Ecologist, Entomologist, Herpetologist, Ichthyologist, Mammalogist, Marine Biologist, Ornithologist.

LOGICAL/MATHEMATICAL

Determine what might cause each of the different types of scientists listed above to choose his or her particular area of study.

VISUAL/SPATIAL

Create a unique symbol or logo to represent each of the different types of scientists given here.

BODY/KINESTHETIC

Prepare a poster that shares information about the different types of scientists and what they study.

MUSICAL/RHYTHMIC

Create an advertising jingle to promote one or more of the science jobs as a potential career choice for students.

INTERPERSONAL

Work with several friends to write a "round robin" letter (that is, each person starts writing and passes the work to others to complete) to a scientist asking questions about his or her work.

INTRAPERSONAL

Decide on the type of science job that has the least appeal to you as a career choice and give reasons for your answer.

Scientific Instruments
Tools of the Scientist

VERBAL/LINGUISTIC
Brainstorm a list of as many different tools as you can think of that are important in scientific study. Consider everything from a microscope to a barometer. Choose one and give a brief verbal report on its purpose and function.

LOGICAL/MATHEMATICAL
Use the list of science tools from the previous activity and classify the items in at least three different ways. Write a paragraph justifying your classification systems.

VISUAL/SPATIAL
Draw a diagram of one of the science tools of special interest to you and label its parts.

BODY/KINESTHETIC
Obtain one or more of the science tools and demonstrate its proper use in a simple "how-to" demonstration.

MUSICAL/RHYTHMIC
Choose one or more of the science tools and write an original lyrical statement using alliteration as your musical device. Example: A microscope meets the eye and magnifies the meager but magical mysteries of the magnificent mantis.

INTERPERSONAL
Work with a small group of peers to determine the five most important or useful scientific tools in today's middle school classroom. Justify your choices.

INTRAPERSONAL
Write a paragraph telling others what your science textbook might say about you to a friend, parent, or teacher.

Environmental Studies

Taking Environmental Concerns Personally

VERBAL/LINGUISTIC
Prepare a short talk that could persuade others that the actions they take as individuals to preserve the environment can really make a difference.

LOGICAL/MATHEMATICAL
Take a look at a selection of environmental problems such as the greenhouse effect, air pollution, ozone depletion, acid rain, and vanishing wildlife. Analyze the problems to determine the relative importance of each one in terms of its danger to safety and health on our planet. Is there a problem that is often overlooked though it is really a major threat? Is there a problem in which you think people put *too much* time and money?

VISUAL/SPATIAL
Create a bright, attention-getting poster that shows some simple things kids can do to help preserve the environment.

BODY/KINESTHETIC
Prepare an active demonstration of a range of cleanup procedures, from simple picking up of trash to the complicated procedures that are sometimes executed by large organizations.

MUSICAL/RHYTHMIC
Create the melody and words for a jingle that could inspire others to work for environmental health.

INTERPERSONAL
Work with classmates to prepare a comprehensive reference list of local organizations that offer help and information to people who are interested in environmental issues. Use the telephone if necessary in order to consult those who can help you prepare the list.

INTRAPERSONAL
How do you feel about the limitations that conserving and preserving the world's resources may place on your life? What would make you feel better about these limitations? Do you think other people feel the way you do? Summarize your thoughts in a short paragraph.

Using Learning Stations as an Instructional Tool

Learning stations come in every size, shape, and color, and can be placed in ordinary or unusual locations. A learning station can be as simple as a bulletin board station that is used by students for extra credit when their regular work is done, or as sophisticated as a series of technology stations around which the entire classroom program is organized. Learning stations can be used for teaching content or practicing skills on a daily basis, weekly basis, monthly basis, or for an entire semester.

The principal importance of a learning station is that it is a physical area where students engage in a variety of learning activities. An effective learning station (1) includes multilevel tasks; (2) offers choices in and alternatives to the tasks it requires; (3) is attractive and motivational; (4) provides clear directions and procedures; (5) accommodates three to five students at one sitting; (6) has flexible time limitations for completion; (7) controls and coordinates movement to and from or between stations; (8) incorporates varied learning styles, modalities, and intelligences; (9) manages student participation through record-keeping strategies; and (10) encourages authentic types of assessment through the use of products and portfolios.

Some of the best formats for learning stations are:

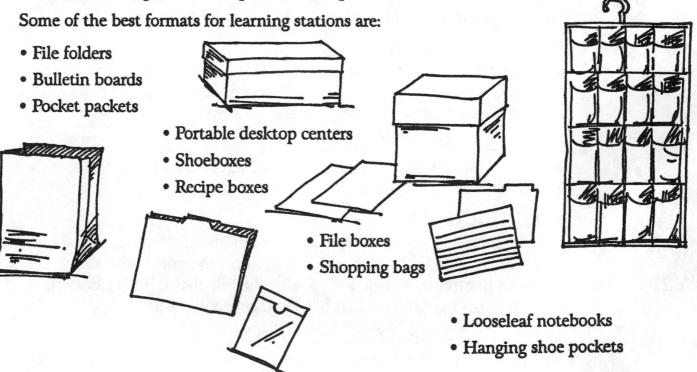

- File folders
- Bulletin boards
- Pocket packets

- Portable desktop centers
- Shoeboxes
- Recipe boxes

- File boxes
- Shopping bags

- Looseleaf notebooks
- Hanging shoe pockets

For more examples and explanations of learning station formats, see *Interdisciplinary Units and Projects for Thematic Instruction* by Imogene Forte and Sandra Schurr, Incentive Publications, 1995.

Some of the most practical ways to use space when setting up learning stations are the following:

Arrange desks in clusters of four or six.

Place an easel between two desks (or place two desks on each side of the easel).

Use bulletin boards or hanging displays in strategic positions.

Use round tables.

Place bookcases at an angle in a corner of the room, adjacent to clustered desks or round tables.

Use backs of bookcases, teacher's desk, or other large pieces of furniture.

Arrange lap boards made of masonite or plywood around a carpeted area where students can sit on the floor.

Some evaluative techniques for use with learning stations that could become products and artifacts for a portfolio are:

- Anecdotal records
- Games, quizzes, puzzles
- Logs and diaries
- Teacher- or student-made tests
- Class or individual charts, graphs
- Checklists
- Tape recordings
- Suggestion boxes
- Scrapbooks or notebooks
- Observation records
- Interviews
- Conferences
- Student rating scales
- Daily progress reports
- Library pockets with individual reporting cards

Finally, here are some things that should be considered before setting up learning stations in the middle level classroom:

1   Decide what you want to teach at each station. Write one or more student objectives. These should be things the student should do in order to show that he or she understands the concept or skill presented.

2   Decide on optional strategies, activities, and tasks for teaching those objectives.

3   Locate all supporting tools and materials for completing the assigned and/or optional tasks. Be sure that students know which materials are included in the station, how to use the materials, and how to care for them.

4   Write specific directions, procedures, and explanations for doing the work at the station. Give students an estimated timetable for completion of the station.

5   Plan for "traffic flow" in relation to other activities that will take place while the station is in use. Plan also for scheduling students into use of the stations. There are many ways to do this. Students can be scheduled to attend each station on a specific rotation. Provided there is room at a new station, students can move on to that station when they are finished with an assigned station. If the stations or station tasks are flexible and portable, students can take them to their seats. Finally, students can sign up for stations based on their interests and/or learning needs.

6   Introduce all station themes or names and the character and major content of each station before students actually begin tackling station activities. Be specific when you tell students what your expectations are in terms of their performance or achievement at each station, and be sure students understand how their achievements will be assessed. As part of this process, provide checkpoints where students may go for help should they forget or misunderstand initial instructions, or where students may review the information presented in this introduction.

Using the Read and Relate Concept as an Instructional Tool

Read and Relate activities require the student to read or review a set of important concepts in a given subject area and then use these concepts as springboards for applying a range of creative or critical thinking skills.

Using the textbook or a favorite set of alternative reference materials, the teacher begins the Read and Relate process by selecting a number of key ideas related to a topic that is being taught as part of an instructional unit. These ideas should be representative of key facts that will be learned by the student. It is also crucial that these ideas lend themselves easily to a number of extended reading, writing, or thinking exercises that can provide opportunities for students to apply the facts in a new and different context.

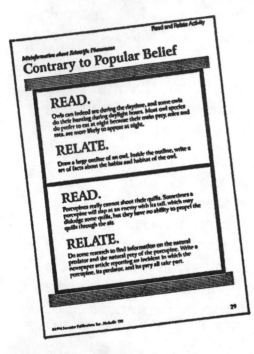

Once the teacher has generated a list, the concepts are written as a series of short, descriptive paragraphs to be reviewed by the student. The paragraphs should be approximately three to five sentences in length, and they should be presented in a logical or sequential manner.

Next, teachers should use Bloom's Taxonomy, Williams' Taxonomy, or any of Gardner's Multiple Intelligences as a basis for developing a follow-up reading, writing, speaking, or thinking activity for each factual paragraph. The activity should require the student to "do something" with the concept in a new and different way. The intent of this instructional strategy is to help the student understand that many important ideas learned in one subject area can be related to ideas in another subject area.

Notice how each descriptive paragraph is followed by a special application challenge for students to complete.

Misinformation about Scientific Phenomena

Contrary to Popular Belief

READ.

Owls can indeed see during the daytime, and some owls do their hunting during daylight hours. Most owl species do prefer to eat at night because their main prey, mice and rats, are more likely to appear at night.

RELATE.

Draw a large outline of an owl. Inside the outline, write a set of facts about the habits and habitat of the owl.

READ.

Porcupines really cannot shoot their quills. Sometimes a porcupine will slap at an enemy with its tail, which may dislodge some quills, but they have no ability to propel the quills through the air.

RELATE.

Do some research to find information on the natural predator and the natural prey of the porcupine. Write a newspaper article reporting an incident in which the porcupine, its predator, and its prey all take part.

Computers

Computer Communication

READ.

Programming a computer means communicating with it in ways it can understand. Using a code of letters, numbers, and symbols called programming language, you tell the computer what to do and how to do it. The machine changes the letters, numbers, and symbols into electrical impulses—its language.

RELATE.

Write a story with one of these titles:

1. A Chip That Made a Mistake
2. An Impulse That Took a Detour
3. The Memory That Got Amnesia
4. The Monitor Who Failed to Respond

READ.

Computers use electricity to do their many jobs, and they work fast. In one second, a computer can perform mathematical operations that would keep twenty people busy all day.

RELATE.

Write a "letter to the editor" telling how a robot replaced you on your summer job, and another letter telling how computers helped you find a new job.

Using Integrated Instructional Strategies to Develop Problem-solving and Higher-order Thinking Skills

Using Bloom's Taxonomy as an Instructional Tool

Bloom's Taxonomy is a well-known model for teaching critical thinking skills in any subject area. Based on the work of Benjamin Bloom, the taxonomy consists of six different thinking levels arranged in a hierarchy of difficulty.

Any student can function at each level of the taxonomy provided the content is appropriate for his or her reading ability. In order for teachers to consistently design lesson plans that incorporate all six levels, they should use the taxonomy to structure all student objectives, all information sessions, all questions, all assigned tasks, and all items on tests.

On the opposite page is a brief summary of the six taxonomy levels with a list of common student behaviors, presented as action verbs, associated with each level. When developing learning tasks and activities around Bloom's Taxonomy, it is important to include in each set at least one activity for each level of the taxonomy. Keep a copy of the Bloom's page in your lesson planning book so it will be handy when you need it.

Bloom's Taxonomy can be used to structure sets of learning tasks, student worksheets, cooperative learning group assignments, and independent study units. On the following pages you will find a collection of learning assignments based on this taxonomy. Topics were selected to be appealing to students and to blend into a middle grades curriculum.

Bloom's Taxonomy of Critical Thought

KNOWLEDGE LEVEL: Learn the information.

Sample Verbs: Define, find, follow directions, identify, know, label, list, memorize, name, quote, read, recall, recite, recognize, select, state, write.

COMPREHENSION LEVEL: Understand the information.

Sample Verbs: Account for, explain, express in other terms, give examples, give in own words, group, infer, interpret, illustrate, paraphrase, recognize, retell, show, simplify, summarize, translate.

APPLICATION LEVEL: Use the information.

Sample Verbs: Apply, compute, construct, construct using, convert (in math), demonstrate, derive, develop, discuss, generalize, interview, investigate, keep records, model, participate, perform, plan, produce, prove (in math), solve, use, utilize.

ANALYSIS LEVEL: Break the information down into its component parts.

Sample Verbs: Analyze, compare, contrast, criticize, debate, determine, diagram, differentiate, discover, draw conclusions, examine, infer, relate, search, sort, survey, take apart, uncover.

SYNTHESIS LEVEL: Put information together in new and different ways.

Sample Verbs: Build, combine, create, design, imagine, invent, make up, produce, propose, present.

EVALUATION LEVEL: Judge the information.

Sample Verbs: Assess, defend, evaluate, grade, judge, measure, perform a critique, rank, recommend, select, test, validate, verify.

Astronomy
Telescope Closeup

KNOWLEDGE

Create a line drawing of a telescope, using reference materials as needed to assist you. Label the parts of the telescope.

COMPREHENSION

In your own words, tell why telescopes are important tools for scientists studying the universe. Tell how telescopes are used by the scientists.

APPLICATION

Construct an outline for an instructional manual that tells about the care and use of a telescope.

SYNTHESIS

Invent a new kind of scientific tool with a name that ends in -*scope*. Write a definition of the new tool, including its intended uses.

ANALYSIS

Compare and contrast a telescope, a microscope, a periscope, and a spectroscope.

EVALUATION

Determine the importance of telescopes in each of the following situations:
- Space exploration
- Military observation
- Birdwatching
- Transoceanic navigation

Petrology

Marvelous Marble

KNOWLEDGE

Make a list of all the ways you can think of that marble is used to improve the quality of people's lives.

COMPREHENSION

Explain how marble is formed, quarried, stored, and shipped for commercial use.

APPLICATION

Prepare a catalog showing drawings of consumer products which are made from marble. Write catalog descriptions and give suggested prices, including shipping costs, for all the items. For each item, calculate the percentage of total cost constituted by the shipping charge.

SYNTHESIS

Locate the chief marble-producing regions of the world on a world map. Determine how some of these regions influenced the lives and works of artists, builders, and traders over the centuries. Give some examples of famous people whose work with marble is well-known and respected.

ANALYSIS

Do you think that in the next few years humans will devise a substitute for marble that will completely replace natural marble? Write an article for a science journal stating your opinion and giving reasons for it.

EVALUATION

Investigate the uses of various materials for some famous works of art. Determine if there are some works for which marble is the very best material.

Conservation

The Earth's Resources

KNOWLEDGE

Finish the sentences below with the appropriate words.

1. A naturally occurring material that can also be replaced naturally and can be used over and over again to produce goods and services is called a _____ _____.

2. A natural resource that is almost impossible to replace is called a _____ _____.

3. _____ is the most common substance on earth, covering three-fourths of the world's surface. It is essential to life and its conservation is of worldwide importance.

4. Coal, oil, natural gas, copper, gold, and silver are _____ _____ and cannot be replaced.

5. _____ _____ are formed from the remains of plants and animals that lived millions of years ago.

6. The three general levels of soil are _____, _____ _____, and _____ _____.

7. The chief benefits of _____ _____ are that it is inexpensive and almost inexhaustible because it is derived from the sun.

8. A person whose occupation is based on making wise use of the world's resources is called a _____.

9. _____ is the process of reusing products that have been previously used and discarded.

10. The uneven distribution of the earth's natural resources makes _____ _____ necessary.

The Earth's Resources

APPLICATION

Write an article for your school newspaper explaining why it is important for people of your age to practice and promote recycling.

COMPREHENSION

Explain how the earth's natural resources help people satisfy both wants and needs and how the natural resources of any geographical area are directly related to the lifestyles and economic opportunities available to people living in the region.

SYNTHESIS

Create a trivia game or a board game containing a set of questions and answers related to the earth's resources and their uses. Example: How does strip mining affect the earth's surface? What are the differences in subsistence farming and commercial farming? Why is it important for new trees to be planted to replace those cut down? Give a positive example and a negative example of how modern technology has influenced the use of natural resources.

ANALYSIS

Develop a poster to show the steps that can be taken by farmers to make sure that the soil remains a renewable rather than a non-renewable natural resource.

EVALUATION

Develop an evaluation form or a checklist that could be used to assess the degree of responsibility members of your class are assuming for protecting the earth's ever-diminishing resources for future generations.

Health

Heart Healthy

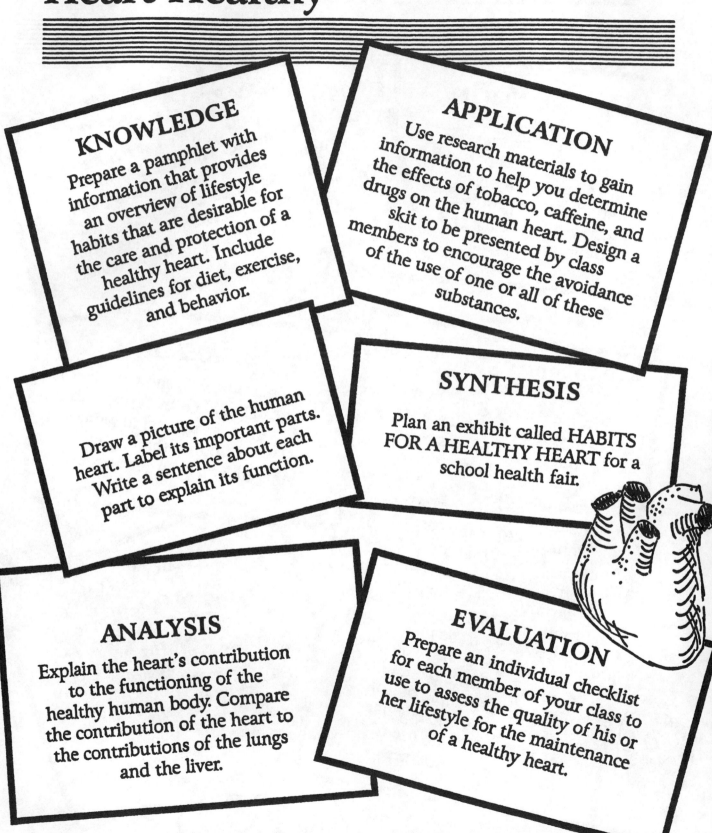

KNOWLEDGE

Prepare a pamphlet with information that provides an overview of lifestyle habits that are desirable for the care and protection of a healthy heart. Include guidelines for diet, exercise, and behavior.

APPLICATION

Use research materials to gain information to help you determine the effects of tobacco, caffeine, and drugs on the human heart. Design a skit to be presented by class members to encourage the avoidance of the use of one or all of these substances.

Draw a picture of the human heart. Label its important parts. Write a sentence about each part to explain its function.

SYNTHESIS

Plan an exhibit called HABITS FOR A HEALTHY HEART for a school health fair.

ANALYSIS

Explain the heart's contribution to the functioning of the healthy human body. Compare the contribution of the heart to the contributions of the lungs and the liver.

EVALUATION

Prepare an individual checklist for each member of your class to use to assess the quality of his or her lifestyle for the maintenance of a healthy heart.

Horticulture

Trees to Know

KNOWLEDGE

List the common names of at least fifty trees that are native to your community.

APPLICATION

Construct a list of questions about trees that can be answered by using science reference materials available in your school. Then construct a second list of questions about trees in your own neighborhood about which you would like to know more. Read your completed list and write beside each question the name of a person you could consult for verbal information to answer your question.

COMPREHENSION

Draw a tree that grows near your home or school. Label its major parts. Find out if the tree bears fruit or flowers and, if so, in which season.

ANALYSIS

Collect available leaves, stems, flowers, fruits, seeds, and/or other products from a particular tree near your school or home. Analyze each product to determine its role in the tree's growth and propagation.

SYNTHESIS

Read the story of Johnny Appleseed and the role he played in planting apple trees for the benefit of future generations. Pretend you are this year's Johnny Appleseed. It is your responsibility to plant trees in your own community to provide one species of tree for citizens of the next century to enjoy. Write a story telling about the trees and how, where, and when you would plant them.

EVALUATION

Write a script for a television program or a videotape to inform others of the different species of trees in your community and to encourage people to help care for and preserve them.

Weather

Hurricane Havoc

KNOWLEDGE

Write a complete definition of the word "hurricane."

COMPREHENSION

Draw a picture to show the possible effects of a hurricane.

APPLICATION

Outline a chapter on natural disasters for a third- or fourth-grade science textbook. Include hurricanes, tornadoes, and earthquakes.

ANALYSIS

Compare the wind speeds that precede a hurricane with the wind speeds that precede a tornado. Write a word problem based on this comparison.

SYNTHESIS

Design a special flyer to be distributed to senior citizens living near oceans to teach them about the origins and dangers of hurricanes. The flyer should explain what people should do in order to protect themselves in the event of a hurricane.

EVALUATION

Devise an authentic assessment product or performance task to evaluate your own knowledge and understanding of the causes and effects of hurricanes.

Eggs
Examine an Egg

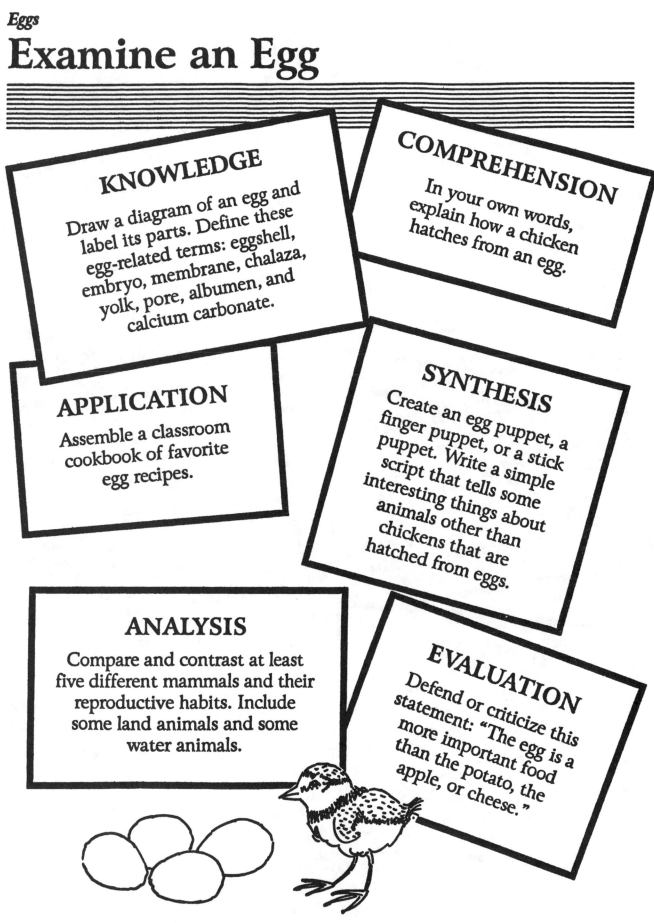

KNOWLEDGE

Draw a diagram of an egg and label its parts. Define these egg-related terms: eggshell, embryo, membrane, chalaza, yolk, pore, albumen, and calcium carbonate.

COMPREHENSION

In your own words, explain how a chicken hatches from an egg.

APPLICATION

Assemble a classroom cookbook of favorite egg recipes.

SYNTHESIS

Create an egg puppet, a finger puppet, or a stick puppet. Write a simple script that tells some interesting things about animals other than chickens that are hatched from eggs.

ANALYSIS

Compare and contrast at least five different mammals and their reproductive habits. Include some land animals and some water animals.

EVALUATION

Defend or criticize this statement: "The egg is a more important food than the potato, the apple, or cheese."

Botany

The Flowering Plants

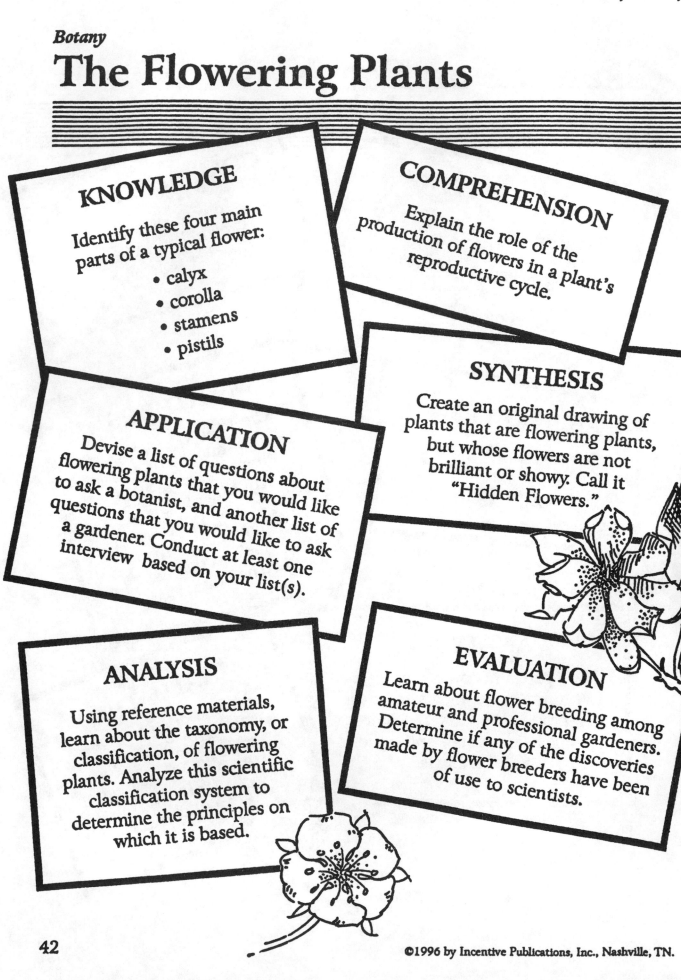

KNOWLEDGE

Identify these four main parts of a typical flower:

- calyx
- corolla
- stamens
- pistils

COMPREHENSION

Explain the role of the production of flowers in a plant's reproductive cycle.

APPLICATION

Devise a list of questions about flowering plants that you would like to ask a botanist, and another list of questions that you would like to ask a gardener. Conduct at least one interview based on your list(s).

SYNTHESIS

Create an original drawing of plants that are flowering plants, but whose flowers are not brilliant or showy. Call it "Hidden Flowers."

ANALYSIS

Using reference materials, learn about the taxonomy, or classification, of flowering plants. Analyze this scientific classification system to determine the principles on which it is based.

EVALUATION

Learn about flower breeding among amateur and professional gardeners. Determine if any of the discoveries made by flower breeders have been of use to scientists.

Chemical Reactions

Chemical Changes

KNOWLEDGE

Identify the following chemical changes:

- Combination of iron with oxygen
- Bonding of two atoms of hydrogen and one of oxygen into a single molecule
- Bonding of one atom of carbon with two atoms of oxygen

COMPREHENSION

In your own words, describe how a common chemical reaction takes place. Then give an example of a substance that undergoes a physical change without undergoing a chemical change.

APPLICATION

Learn about the many artificial products that chemists have developed. Make an analysis of your findings to determine if people's lives have been improved by many of these developments.

SYNTHESIS

Invent a new chemical compound. Include the elements from which it is made, a diagram of its structure, a name, and a description of its properties.

ANALYSIS

Make an analysis of your daily routine to see how much of what you do includes or requires some kind of chemical reaction.

EVALUATION

Determine the importance of having some knowledge of simple chemical reactions in everyday life.

Using Williams' Taxonomy as an Instructional Tool

Williams' Taxonomy is another important model to use when teaching thinking skills. While Bloom's Taxonomy is used for teaching critical thinking skills, Williams' Taxonomy is used for teaching creative thinking skills.

Although there is a relationship between these two models, and even some overlap, it should be noted that critical thinking tends to be more reactive and vertical in nature while creative thinking tends to be more proactive and lateral in nature. Another way of saying this is that critical thinking tends to involve tasks that are logical, rational, sequential, analytical, and convergent. Creative thinking, on the other hand, tends to involve tasks that are spatial, flexible, spontaneous, analogical, and divergent. Critical thinking is "left brain" thinking while creative thinking is "right brain" thinking.

Williams' Taxonomy has eight levels, also arranged in a hierarchy, with certain types of student behavior associated with each level. The first four levels of the Williams' model are cognitive in nature while the last four levels are affective in nature.

It is strongly suggested that a teacher keep a copy of Williams' Taxonomy in the lesson plan book so that the levels and behaviors can be an integral part of most lesson plans and student assignments. On the opposite page is a brief overview of the levels in Williams' Taxonomy. Each level is accompanied by a few cue words to be used to trigger student responses to a given creative stimulus or challenge.

The following pages offer a wide variety of student worksheets, assignments, independent study guides, or group problem-solving tasks, covering many different content areas appropriate for middle grade classrooms.

44

Williams' Taxonomy of Creative Thought

FLUENCY

Enables the learner to generate a great many ideas, related answers, or choices in a given situation.

Sample Cue Words: Generating oodles, lots, many ideas.

FLEXIBILITY

Lets the learner change everyday objects to generate a variety of categories by taking detours and varying sizes, shapes, quantities, time limits, requirements, objectives, or dimensions in a given situation.

Sample Cue Words: Generating varied, different, alternative ideas.

ORIGINALITY

Causes the learner to seek new ideas by suggesting unusual twists to change content or by coming up with clever responses to a given situation.

Sample Cue Words: Generating unusual, unique, new ideas.

ELABORATION

Helps the learner stretch by expanding, enlarging, enriching, or embellishing possibilities that build on previous thoughts or ideas.

Sample Cue Words: Generating enriched, embellished, expanded ideas.

RISK TAKING

Enables the learner to deal with the unknown by taking chances, experimenting with new ideas, or trying new challenges.

Sample Cue Words: Experimenting with and exploring ideas.

COMPLEXITY

Permits the learner to create structure in an unstructured setting or to build a logical order in a given situation.

Sample Cue Words: Improving and explaining ideas.

CURIOSITY

Encourages the learner to follow a hunch, question alternatives, ponder outcomes, and wonder about options in a given situation.

Sample Cue Words: Pondering and questioning ideas.

IMAGINATION

Allows the learner to visualize possibilities, build images in his or her mind, picture new objects, or reach beyond the limits of the practical.

Sample Cue Words: Visualizing and fantasizing ideas

Living Organisms
That's Life

 ## FLUENCY
Think of the characteristics that distinguish a living thing from a nonliving thing. List as many of these characteristics as you can.

 ## FLEXIBILITY
Devise a classification system for living things based on the fact that some of the characteristics of living things show themselves in different ways in different kinds of organisms.

 ## ORIGINALITY
Write a description of life as if you had to explain life to a nonliving thing.

ELABORATION
Explain how scientists in the field of biology rely on methods and discoveries of scientists in other fields in order to do their work.

 ## RISK TAKING
Tell how you feel about the possible benefits and the potential dangers of modern advances in genetic engineering.

 ## COMPLEXITY
Discuss the issues involved in the work of a scientist whose discoveries improve some lives, but whose work also harms some living things through experiments on which the work is based.

CURIOSITY
What questions would you like to ask a biologist in order to learn about a typical day in the life of a biologist?

IMAGINATION
Write a brief imaginative account of Marcello Malpighi's first view of the movement of blood through capillaries with a microscope.

Meteorologists

Measuring and Predicting

 FLUENCY
Make as complete a list as you can of the many things meteorologists measure in order to predict the weather.

 FLEXIBILITY
Classify the conditions and substances measured by meteorologists according to how they are measured.

 ORIGINALITY
Meteorologists have experimented with making rain by cloud seeding. Invent a technique for producing another type of weather.

 ELABORATION
Expand on your Fluency and Flexibility lists by adding as many scientific instruments that measure weather and atmospheric conditions as you can.

 RISK TAKING
Tell if you have ever been angry with a weather forecaster because an incorrect forecast affected your plans.

 COMPLEXITY
Explain some of the reasons that weather forecasting must be inaccurate to some degree.

 CURIOSITY
What would you like to ask a meteorologist about how computers are used in meteorology?

IMAGINATION
Write an account of an international incident provoked by a weather satellite's inadvertent detection of something other than simple weather conditions.

Desert Life
Animals of the Desert

 FLUENCY
List as many animals that are native to the desert as you can.

 FLEXIBILITY
Classify at least twenty desert animals according to size and/or physical characteristics.

 ORIGINALITY
Select one desert animal that is of particular interest to you and draw a series of pictures to show a typical day in its life.

 ELABORATION
Elaborate on this starter statement: "Animals of the desert contribute to the world's economy in the following ways . . ."

 RISK TAKING
Write a brief essay to summarize your feelings about the need to identify and protect endangered desert animals. Do you think too much or too little of your country's resources are devoted to saving endangered plant and animal species?

 COMPLEXITY
Examine reference materials that have information on desert climate to determine how the climatic conditions affect the food chain and life cycles of desert animals.

 CURIOSITY
Develop a list of questions about desert animals that you would like to ask a professional authority on desert life.

IMAGINATION
Visualize yourself as a famous scientist assigned to develop a television documentary on animals of the desert. As a part of your assignment, you will live and work in the desert for six months. Outline the script for the program.

Ways of Telling Time

Time through the Ages

 FLUENCY
Draw pictures of as many things as you can think of that have helped people measure time. Label the pictures.

 FLEXIBILITY
Arrange the timekeeping devices according to a classification system of your invention.

 ORIGINALITY
Describe ways people of today might adapt sundials, fire clocks, or water clocks to tell time in unique situations.

 ELABORATION
Expand on the following statement and write an essay or a poem based on your thinking. "Time is the most valuable thing a person can spend."

 RISK TAKING
Devise a timeline to show the sequence and relationships of the major events of your life.

 COMPLEXITY
Explain how mechanical devices for telling time have affected scientific research and development in this century.

 CURIOSITY
Find out how ancient people watched the night sky to devise one of the earliest systems for telling time.

 IMAGINATION
Invent a new and unusual timepiece for each of the following workers: an astronaut, an orchestra conductor, a long-distance runner, a deep-sea diver.

Electricity
Electric Power

FLUENCY
Make an illustrated list of all the items in your home that use electricity.

FLEXIBILITY
Classify your list of electrical items in at least three different ways.

 ORIGINALITY
Find out how electricity works and design a flow chart to show your findings.

ELABORATION
Develop a glossary of ten to fifteen words related to the generation and distribution of electrical power. Use these words in a wordfind or crossword puzzle.

RISK TAKING
List all the ways you can think of that you and your family waste electricity, and all the ways you can think of that you conserve electricity in your home. Devise a scale to determine your family's rating as conservationists.

 COMPLEXITY
Interview the adults in your home to determine which of the electrical products in use by your family today were not available to them as children. Create a timeline to show the discovery of electricity and the development of its use.

CURIOSITY
Make a list of ten questions related to electricity for which you would like to find answers. Beside each question, list the resource you would use to find the answer (such as resource person's name, encyclopedia, computer program, videotape, magazine, newspaper).

 IMAGINATION
Predict the ways the use of electricity in the home will be affected by the development of high technology in future years. Write a newspaper article presenting your projections.

Fruit

Facts about Fruits

 FLUENCY
List as many fruits that can be purchased in your local grocery store or produce market as you can think of in three minutes.

 FLEXIBILITY
Classify the fruits on your list according to the ways the plants reproduce themselves. Use a circle graph to show your findings.

 ORIGINALITY
Invent an unusual recipe that calls for fruit as the main ingredient. Give complete directions for preparation and serving.

 ELABORATION
Defend or criticize the following statement: "An apple a day keeps the doctor away."

 RISK TAKING
Create a dance that portrays the harvesting, preparation, serving, and eating of a fruit of your choice.

 COMPLEXITY
Analyze a television commercial or a newspaper or magazine advertisement that advertises a particular fruit to determine if and how the producers portray the benefits of the fruit accurately or if and how they exaggerate the health benefits to exploit the consumer.

 CURIOSITY
Write a story explaining and expanding on how fruits have played a role in world history or in shaping a particular community's culture. Illustrate your story.

IMAGINATION
Imagine what a pineapple might say to a grapefruit, a papaya, and a banana when they find themselves in the same fruit bowl in a health food restaurant.

Lungs

Learning about Lungs

 FLUENCY
List all the characteristics of lungs that you can, including function, location, size, shape, and color.

 FLEXIBILITY
Explore how the function of the lungs is related to the functions of other organs in the body.

 ORIGINALITY
Think of a way to construct a model of the lungs that will show how the lungs expand and contract.

 ELABORATION
Expand on your list of lung characteristics by listing the scientific names of various parts of the lungs.

 RISK TAKING
Describe the feelings you had when you saw a picture of the lungs of a person who had been smoking for years.

 COMPLEXITY
There has been conflict between people who fight for "smokers' rights" and people who feel that interfering with a person's right to smoke is justified because it protects other people who want to keep their lungs healthy. What is your view of the issues involved in this controversy?

 CURIOSITY
If you could talk to a surgeon who has performed operations on human lungs, what would you like to ask him or her? What would you like to know about such a surgical procedure?

 IMAGINATION
Write a brief science fiction scenario that describes how people will survive if the air in the future world becomes too polluted for people to breathe with their lungs in the normal way.

Shells

A Selection of Shells

 FLUENCY
List as many different types of shells as you can.

 FLEXIBILITY
Classify your list according to the uses that could be made of these different types of shells.

 ORIGINALITY
Create a wrapping paper, wallpaper, or writing paper design using a shell motif.

 ELABORATION
What kinds of characteristics of a living animal can you infer from examining its shell after the animal is gone?

 RISK TAKING
Tell how you feel about people who pick up shells in protected areas where collecting shells and wildlife is prohibited.

 COMPLEXITY
Think of some ways to compare a creature with a shell to some human beings. Use metaphors or other descriptive language.

 CURIOSITY
Imagine you know a zoologist who has a special interest in shell-producing animals. What questions would you like to ask this scientist in order to learn more about the lives of such animals?

IMAGINATION
Design an unusual and effective way to organize collections of shells for display.

Astronomy

Consider the Cosmos

 FLUENCY
List as many different types of celestial bodies as you can. Include unusual types as well as well-known celestial bodies such as planets and stars.

 FLEXIBILITY
Think of a classification system for the items in your list. You may consider temperature, size, distances, or any other attributes for your system.

 ORIGINALITY
Come up with a different ending to the story of the Inquisition of Galileo Galilei.

 ELABORATION
Expand on this statement: "Astronomy compels the soul to look upwards and leads us from this world to another."—Plato

 RISK TAKING
Describe what you think is at the end of the universe.

 COMPLEXITY
Explain the Theory of Relativity the best way you can, and tell if you think knowledge of this theory has been important in the life of the average person.

CURIOSITY
If you could meet an astronaut who has been in outer space, what would you want to know about his or her life?

 IMAGINATION
Write a science fiction story about space travel. Include some scientific facts in your story.

Energy Resources

Sources of Power

 FLUENCY
List as many sources of energy as you can.

 FLEXIBILITY
Devise a system of classification for your energy list. Think about safety, availability, cost, and other considerations when you are devising your system.

 ORIGINALITY
Invent a means of producing energy that has advantages over traditional energy production as well as over relatively new developments such as solar power. Try to invent a means that has some scientific basis.

 ELABORATION
Explain how some of the energy sources in your original list are harnessed.

 RISK TAKING
Tell if you have ever resented the fact that it is often necessary to conserve energy.

 COMPLEXITY
Why do some people take energy crises seriously, while others believe the crises are often fabricated?

 CURIOSITY
What would you like to ask a geologist about energy resources today?

IMAGINATION
Imagine what the world would be like if someone discovered a renewable source of energy that was free and available to all.

Blood

Life-giving Blood

 FLUENCY
List all the characteristics of blood that you know.

 FLEXIBILITY
Classify the characteristics in your list according to a system of your own devising.

ORIGINALITY
Make up a new word for "blood."

 ELABORATION
Expand on your list of blood characteristics by giving the scientific names of the various components of blood.

 RISK TAKING
Tell how you feel about donating blood.

 COMPLEXITY
Discuss the issues involved in balancing a person's right to privacy against the need to maintain a safe blood supply for medical purposes.

CURIOSITY
What would you like to ask a nurse or doctor about the importance of the blood supply?

 IMAGINATION
Describe an imaginary trip taken by a microscopic creature through the blood vessels of a human being.

Medicinal Plants

Plants That Are Good for You

 FLUENCY
List as many plants as you can that are used for medical purposes.

 FLEXIBILITY
Classify the plants on your list according to their specific medicinal uses.

 ORIGINALITY
Invent a new medicine derived from plant sources. Tell how it is extracted, prepared, and administered, and the condition for which it is used. Describe its effects.

ELABORATION
Add to your list of medicinal plants a selection of plants that are used for other purposes such as fertilizer and other plant products.

 RISK TAKING
Tell about a time you refused to take your medicine.

COMPLEXITY
Explore the issues involved in the preservation of the rain forest. Include a look at how rain forest destruction could have a harmful effect on the supply of plant-derived medicines.

 CURIOSITY
Make a list of questions to ask an herbalist in order to discover his or her opinion of modern medicine and how it compares to traditional herbal medicine.

 IMAGINATION
Imagine a story about a person with a disease that can be cured only by a rare plant. What does this person do in order to procure the plant?

Using Investigation Cards as an Instructional Tool

Investigation Cards provide a tool for differentiating instruction in a classroom of diverse abilities, interests, and cultures. The cards are designed around Bloom's Taxonomy of Cognitive Development, with three tasks written for each of the six levels. This makes Investigation Cards helpful in "smuggling thinking skills into the curriculum."

Investigation Cards can be used in several ways. Teachers can assign cards to students, or students can select their own cards. Teachers can require students to complete at least one card at each level of the taxonomy, or they can require students to complete cards at any given level or levels of the taxonomy. Teachers can also assign Investigation Cards to cooperative learning groups, with each group having the same set of cards, or each group working on a different set. Finally, Investigation Cards make excellent homework assignments, enrichment assignments, or assignments for students with special needs.

You will need a supply of blank 4" x 6" file cards to prepare the Investigation Cards. Make three copies of each page of graphic cards in this book. Cut apart the cards on the dotted lines and paste each one on the back of one of the 4" x 6" file cards. Then make a copy of each page of task cards, cut apart the cards on the dotted lines, and paste each task card on the back of the appropriate graphic card. If time permits, color the graphics and laminate the set of Investigation Cards for extended use. If time is limited, you may make copies of the task cards alone, cut them apart, and give each student or group of students the paper task cards for immediate use.

Students and teachers can make additional sets of Investigation Cards on topics of their choice by following these simple steps:

1 Select an object or topic of interest to you in your subject area that lends itself to the Investigation Card concept.

2 Collect information associated with your object or topic and use this information to identify major terms, background data, or major concepts related to your Investigation Card theme.

3 Write three different questions, tasks, challenges, or activities for each level of Bloom's Taxonomy using the object or topic as the springboard for ideas. The Bloom Cue Charts found in three Incentive Publications books—*The Definitive Middle School Guide; Tools, Treasures, and Measures;* and *Science Mind Stretchers*—offer excellent guidance for this purpose.

SCIENCE

Investigate a Camera

©1996 Incentive Publications, Inc., Nashville, TN. GRAPHIC CARD

SCIENCE

Investigate a Camera

©1996 Incentive Publications, Inc., Nashville, TN. GRAPHIC CARD

SCIENCE

Investigate a Camera

©1996 Incentive Publications, Inc., Nashville, TN. GRAPHIC CARD

SCIENCE

Investigate a Camera

©1996 Incentive Publications, Inc., Nashville, TN. GRAPHIC CARD

SCIENCE

Investigate a Camera

©1996 Incentive Publications, Inc., Nashville, TN. GRAPHIC CARD

SCIENCE

Investigate a Camera

©1996 Incentive Publications, Inc., Nashville, TN. GRAPHIC CARD

KNOWLEDGE

Draw an outline and/or cutaway view of a camera and label these parts: lens, shutter, viewfinder, aperture, shutter release, film cassette insert, and film rewind/advance button.

TASK CARD

Investigate a Camera

COMPREHENSION

Give an explanation of how a camera takes pictures.

TASK CARD

Investigate a Camera

KNOWLEDGE

Define the function of each of the major parts of the camera.

TASK CARD

Investigate a Camera

COMPREHENSION

Describe the way in which a flash works.

TASK CARD

Investigate a Camera

KNOWLEDGE

Tell who is responsible for inventing the first camera and when and where it was invented.

TASK CARD

Investigate a Camera

COMPREHENSION

Describe the function of a light meter.

TASK CARD

Investigate a Camera

APPLICATION

Construct a photoessay on a topic of your choice. Each photograph in your essay should be accompanied by a descriptive paragraph.

TASK CARD

Investigate a Camera

ANALYSIS

Draw conclusions about what life would be like if memories were only retained for a year.

TASK CARD

Investigate a Camera

APPLICATION

Construct a "photostory." Write your fictional piece, including accompanying photographs.

TASK CARD

Investigate a Camera

ANALYSIS

Infer ways that the human eye functions much like a camera.

TASK CARD

Investigate a Camera

APPLICATION

Construct a "photoautobiography." Include an outline that summarizes the organization of your photo album. Prepare an oral talk so you can share the contents of your photo album.

TASK CARD

Investigate a Camera

ANALYSIS

Compare and contrast a camera, a camcorder, and a slide projector. How are these pieces of equipment alike and how are they different?

TASK CARD

Investigate a Camera

SYNTHESIS

Imagine what a camera would say to a roll of film, a darkroom, and a flashcube.

TASK CARD

Investigate a Camera

EVALUATION

Debate whether or not photography is an art form.

TASK CARD

Investigate a Camera

SYNTHESIS

Pretend you are a famous underwater photographer. Draw a picture of an extraordinary underwater scene that you want to capture on film.

TASK CARD

Investigate a Camera

EVALUATION

Rank the following photography roles according to which is of most benefit to society: crime photographer, portrait photographer, or nature photographer. Explain your ranking.

TASK CARD

Investigate a Camera

SYNTHESIS

Write a short story whose final line reads: "A picture is worth a thousand words."

TASK CARD

Investigate a Camera

EVALUATION

Defend or criticize this statement: "Beauty is in the eye of the beholder."

TASK CARD

Investigate a Camera

KNOWLEDGE

List as many things as you can think of that fly.

TASK CARD

Investigate Flight

COMPREHENSION

Summarize the contributions of these individuals to the world of flight: Orville and Wilbur Wright, Charles Lindbergh, Amelia Earhart, and Otto Lilienthal.

TASK CARD

Investigate Flight

KNOWLEDGE

Define these flight-related words: lift, thrust, drag, gravity.

TASK CARD

Investigate Flight

COMPREHENSION

Explain Bernouilli's Principle and tell how it relates to flight.

TASK CARD

Investigate Flight

KNOWLEDGE

Draw an outline of an airplane and label these parts: cockpit, wing, propeller, fuselage, elevator, tailfin, rudder, and aileron.

TASK CARD

Investigate Flight

COMPREHENSION

Describe how a bird flies.

TASK CARD

Investigate Flight

APPLICATION

Construct a series of model airplanes and stage an airplane flying contest with your classmates.

TASK CARD

Investigate Flight

ANALYSIS

Compare and contrast a glider, hot air balloon, and a kite.

TASK CARD

Investigate Flight

APPLICATION

Construct a series of model insects from tissue paper, plastic bags, cardboard, straws, and thin wire and use these to demonstrate a principle of flight.

TASK CARD

Investigate Flight

ANALYSIS

Classify your list of things that can fly from the Knowledge Level task.

TASK CARD

Investigate Flight

APPLICATION

Construct a parachute using string, plastic bags, and metal washers to show how parachutes can be used to float people and objects safely to the ground.

TASK CARD

Investigate Flight

ANALYSIS

Discover the similarities between a seed in flight and a helicopter or parachute in flight.

TASK CARD

Investigate Flight

SYNTHESIS

Develop an original and colorful design for a hot air balloon.

TASK CARD

Investigate Flight

EVALUATION

Defend or negate this statement: "Flying is the safest form of transportation."

TASK CARD

Investigate Flight

SYNTHESIS

Design an experiment to demonstrate one or more of the principles of flight.

TASK CARD

Investigate Flight

EVALUATION

Do you agree or disagree with the following statement by Archimedes?

"There is no 'nothing' because where there is nothing there is air."

TASK CARD

Investigate Flight

SYNTHESIS

Create a "flight of the imagination."

TASK CARD

Investigate Flight

EVALUATION

Justify the amount of money spent by the United States on the space program.

TASK CARD

Investigate Flight

SCIENCE

Investigate a
Weather Map

GRAPHIC CARD

SCIENCE

Investigate a
Weather Map

GRAPHIC CARD

SCIENCE

Investigate a
Weather Map

GRAPHIC CARD

SCIENCE

Investigate a
Weather Map

GRAPHIC CARD

SCIENCE

Investigate a
Weather Map

GRAPHIC CARD

SCIENCE

Investigate a
Weather Map

GRAPHIC CARD

KNOWLEDGE

List the types of information found on your weather map.

TASK CARD

Investigate a Weather Map

COMPREHENSION

Explain the concept of "forecast" in your own words.

TASK CARD

Investigate a Weather Map

KNOWLEDGE

Locate your city and identify the weather conditions for today.

TASK CARD

Investigate a Weather Map

COMPREHENSION

Describe the type of weather most commonly associated with fronts.

TASK CARD

Investigate a Weather Map

KNOWLEDGE

Draw symbols commonly used for the following: high pressure area, low pressure area, warm front, cold front, stationary front, showers, rain, ice, flurries, sunshine, and snow.

TASK CARD

Investigate a Weather Map

COMPREHENSION

What accounts for "irregular bands" of temperature across the country?

TASK CARD

Investigate a Weather Map

APPLICATION

Make a list of questions you might want to ask a meteorologist.

TASK CARD

Investigate a Weather Map

ANALYSIS

Classify the different types of cloud formations and relate them to weather conditions.

TASK CARD

Investigate a Weather Map

APPLICATION

Collect information about careers related to the weather. Present your information in graphic form.

TASK CARD

Investigate a Weather Map

ANALYSIS

Make inferences about the skills and the training that are required of a weather forecaster.

TASK CARD

Investigate a Weather Map

APPLICATION

Use today's newspaper weather map to produce a short, informative weather report for your class.

TASK CARD

Investigate a Weather Map

ANALYSIS

Compare and contrast the weather conditions that generally exist in three different parts of the country, such as the far west (Washington), the far east (New York), and the southeast (Florida).

TASK CARD

Investigate a Weather Map

SYNTHESIS

Write a creative story about "the day it rained cats and dogs."

TASK CARD

Investigate a Weather Map

EVALUATION

Consider how your life would be affected if there were suddenly no reliable weather predictions and information available to you.

TASK CARD

Investigate a Weather Map

SYNTHESIS

Create a travel brochure describing the details and benefits of taking "a vacation on a cloud."

TASK CARD

Investigate a Weather Map

EVALUATION

Determine the value of weather forecasting to the following individuals: Farmer, Merchant, Homeowner, Vacationer, Airline Pilot, Traveling Salesman, and Fisherman. Determine which individuals are most vulnerable and give reasons for your choices.

TASK CARD

Investigate a Weather Map

SYNTHESIS

Design a greeting card with a message that reflects a weather theme, pun, joke, or riddle.

TASK CARD

Investigate a Weather Map

EVALUATION

Defend or criticize this statement:

"A hurricane is worse than an earthquake."

TASK CARD

Investigate a Weather Map

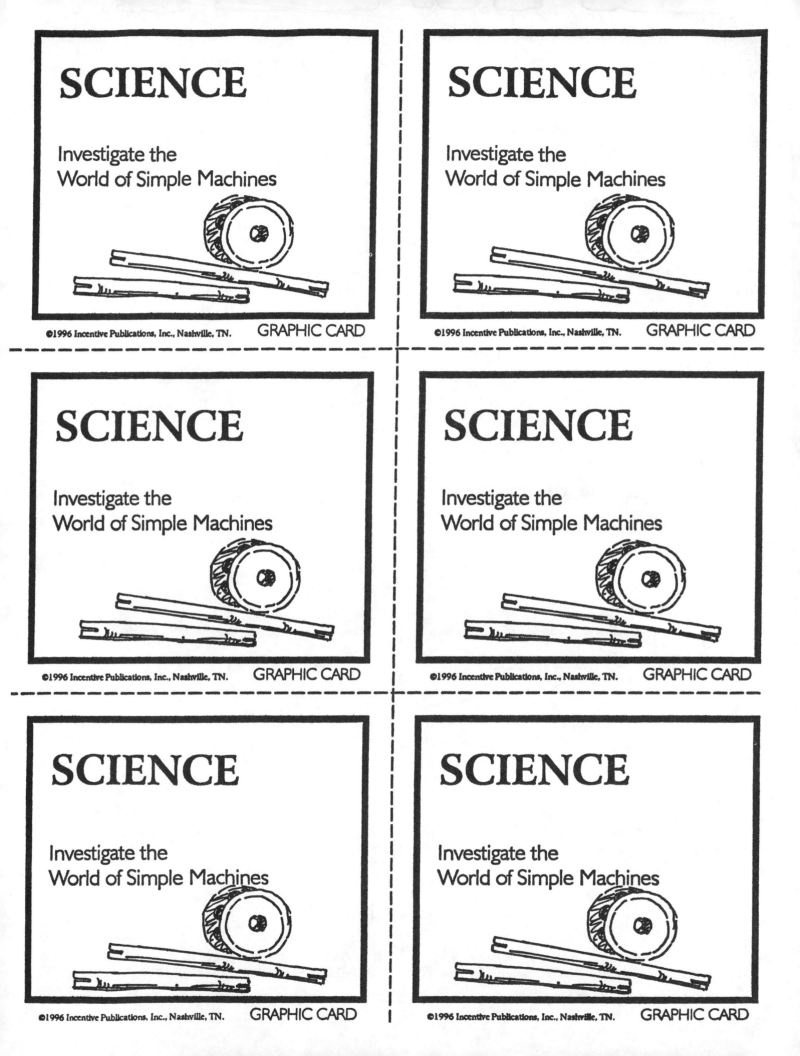

SCIENCE

Investigate the
World of Simple Machines

GRAPHIC CARD

SCIENCE

Investigate the
World of Simple Machines

GRAPHIC CARD

SCIENCE

Investigate the
World of Simple Machines

GRAPHIC CARD

SCIENCE

Investigate the
World of Simple Machines

GRAPHIC CARD

SCIENCE

Investigate the
World of Simple Machines

GRAPHIC CARD

SCIENCE

Investigate the
World of Simple Machines

GRAPHIC CARD

KNOWLEDGE

List the six simple machines and the special attributes of each one.

TASK CARD

Investigate the World of Simple Machines

COMPREHENSION

Explain the basic purpose and/ or function of each simple machine.

TASK CARD

Investigate the World of Simple Machines

KNOWLEDGE

Draw a simple diagram of each of the simple machine types.

TASK CARD

Investigate the World of Simple Machines

COMPREHENSION

Summarize the ways that simple machines help us work.

TASK CARD

Investigate the World of Simple Machines

KNOWLEDGE

Make a list of the simple machines that you commonly find in each room of your dwelling.

TASK CARD

Investigate the World of Simple Machines

COMPREHENSION

Describe a compound machine and give examples of several compound machines that you find at school.

TASK CARD

Investigate the World of Simple Machines

APPLICATION

Construct one or more simple machines from tinker toys, erector sets, or other toy building materials.

TASK CARD

Investigate the World of Simple Machines

ANALYSIS

Compare and contrast the concept of work as it applies to the world of "simple machines" to its application to the world of "careers." How are these concepts alike and how are they different?

TASK CARD

Investigate the World of Simple Machines

APPLICATION

Collect a variety of carpentry tools and demonstrate how they operate as applications of one or more simple machines in action.

TASK CARD

Investigate the World of Simple Machines

ANALYSIS

Predict what your life would be like if you had to go through a day without the use of any simple machine.

TASK CARD

Investigate the World of Simple Machines

APPLICATION

Use a set of building tools to make something out of wood, or use a set of cooking tools to make something good to eat, or use a set of dressmaking/ handworking tools to make something nice to wear.

TASK CARD

Investigate the World of Simple Machines

ANALYSIS

Draw conclusions about how one or more of the simple machines came into existence.

TASK CARD

Investigate the World of Simple Machines

SYNTHESIS

Create a complicated machine that does something unusual or unique. Name the machine, draw it, and describe how it works.

TASK CARD

Investigate the World of Simple Machines

EVALUATION

Defend or negate this statement: "Machines have both enriched our lives and complicated our lives."

TASK CARD

Investigate the World of Simple Machines

SYNTHESIS

Design a robot that would complete school and household tasks that you dislike. Explain what it does and how it works.

TASK CARD

Investigate the World of Simple Machines

EVALUATION

Rank ten simple or compound machines that you have in your home according to their personal value to you. Make 1 the most valuable and 10 the least valuable. Give reasons for your first and last choices.

TASK CARD

Investigate the World of Simple Machines

SYNTHESIS

Invent a machine for the year 2050 that will improve the world for humankind. Write about it in a newspaper article.

TASK CARD

Investigate the World of Simple Machines

EVALUATION

Judge whether the human body is a type of machine. Validate your position with specific arguments and examples.

TASK CARD

Investigate the World of Simple Machines

SCIENCE

Investigate the Beach

©1996 Incentive Publications, Inc., Nashville, TN. GRAPHIC CARD

SCIENCE

Investigate the Beach

©1996 Incentive Publications, Inc., Nashville, TN. GRAPHIC CARD

SCIENCE

Investigate the Beach

©1996 Incentive Publications, Inc., Nashville, TN. GRAPHIC CARD

SCIENCE

Investigate the Beach

©1996 Incentive Publications, Inc., Nashville, TN. GRAPHIC CARD

SCIENCE

Investigate the Beach

©1996 Incentive Publications, Inc., Nashville, TN. GRAPHIC CARD

SCIENCE

Investigate the Beach

©1996 Incentive Publications, Inc., Nashville, TN. GRAPHIC CARD

KNOWLEDGE

List ten things you would want to take with you to spend a productive day at the beach.

TASK CARD

Investigate the Beach

COMPREHENSION

Explain the dangers of a sunburn.

TASK CARD

Investigate the Beach

KNOWLEDGE

List five different things you could observe or learn from spending a day at the beach.

TASK CARD

Investigate the Beach

COMPREHENSION

Illustrate a beach scene. Include in your picture the ocean, the shore, the sand, the shells, and evidence of sea life.

TASK CARD

Investigate the Beach

KNOWLEDGE

Define these beach-related words: ocean, shore, waves, tides, currents, and surf.

TASK CARD

Investigate the Beach

COMPREHENSION

Discuss the dangers that might exist in the ocean and/or on the beach.

TASK CARD

Investigate the Beach

APPLICATION

Interview a person whose career is connected with the beach. Consider a fisherman, lifeguard, marine biologist, or member of the coast guard.

TASK CARD

Investigate the Beach

ANALYSIS

Compare and contrast the beach environment with the mountain environment.

TASK CARD

Investigate the Beach

APPLICATION

Construct a clay model of a sea creature.

TASK CARD

Investigate the Beach

ANALYSIS

Form generalizations about the advantages and disadvantages of living on the beach.

TASK CARD

Investigate the Beach

APPLICATION

Predict what will happen to marine life if we continue to pollute the oceans.

TASK CARD

Investigate the Beach

ANALYSIS

Examine the changes in temperature of beach sand during a 24-hour period of time.

TASK CARD

Investigate the Beach

SYNTHESIS

Create an original poem about the beach. Consider composing the poem in one of these forms: haiku, diamante, limerick, free verse, or tanka.

TASK CARD

Investigate the Beach

EVALUATION

Choose any beach in the southeastern United States that you would most like to visit. Establish criteria for making this choice and defend your final selection.

TASK CARD

Investigate the Beach

SYNTHESIS

Formulate five questions that you would want to ask an environmentalist about our coastal waters and shores.

TASK CARD

Investigate the Beach

EVALUATION

Rank the following lifestyles as being most desirable for a family, with 1 being your first choice and 4 your last choice. Give reasons for your ranking. Lifestyle choices: living on the beach, in the mountains, on a rural farm in the plains, or in the desert.

TASK CARD

Investigate the Beach

SYNTHESIS

Imagine you are a seagull. Describe your typical day at the beach.

TASK CARD

Investigate the Beach

EVALUATION

Recommend a beach vacation for tourists. Justify your recommendation.

TASK CARD

Investigate the Beach

Using Calendars as an Instructional Tool

Contemporary calendars come in all colors, shapes, and sizes. They cover a wide range of themes and messages, often providing the user with much information for thought and motivation for action. A calendar is considered by many to be an art form and a teaching tool as well as a time management aid. Visit a book store, a gift shop, or the card section of a drug store and you will find calendars for everyone from "cat owners" and "movie buffs" to "Snoopy fans" and "nature lovers." Museums often carry calendars on educational topics.

The calendars on the following pages were designed to be used as mini-interdisciplinary units. The activities were chosen to:

- develop skills;
- introduce new concepts;
- stimulate curiosity; and
- present challenges.

These calendar tasks can be used as:

- enrichment;
- homework;
- extra-credit assignments; or
- an addition to the traditional curriculum.

A wide variety of instructional springboards are included for each day of a typical month. Students can:

- complete each day's task as given;
- select one task to complete each week;
- be assigned a particular set of tasks by the teacher; or
- complete the tasks collaboratively with a group of peers.

79

One way to introduce the use of calendars as an instructional tool in the classroom is to have students bring in favorite calendars from home or solicit discarded calendars from retail outlets. Display these calendars and use them as the basis for group discussions and/or student observations. Some starter questions or tasks might be:

1 Who would buy this calendar and why?

2 What could one learn by using this calendar?

3 How are graphics, color, layout, and design used to enhance the theme and appeal of this calendar?

4 Why is a calendar considered by some people to be a "form of modern art"?

5 Why would someone want to collect calendars? What could you do with a bunch of old calendars?

6 Research the history of the calendar. Who invented it and for what purpose?

7 If you were going to create an original calendar, what theme or topic would you choose? Develop your idea into a report, a project, or a display with a calendar format.

8 What would life be like without calendars to help us keep track of time, dates, and events?

State Parks as Conservation Agents

1 List as many state parks found in your state as you can.	**2** Rank the state parks according to the extent to which each one keeps valuable natural resources from being exploited.	**3** Describe and sketch the major natural resources of your favorite state park.	**4** Estimate the distance (in miles) from your home to the nearest state park. Use a map to check the accuracy of your estimate.	**5** Select a state park you would like to visit and write a paragraph describing the natural resources you would expect to find there.
6 Write down three facts and three opinions about conservation of natural resources at a park of your choice.	**7** Design a brochure that features the major attractions of your state's parks.	**8** Expand on this statement: "Conservation does not mean the locking up of our natural resources, nor a hindrance to progress in any direction. It means only wise, careful use." —Mary Huston Gregory	**9** Design a picture postcard for a state park in a part of the state other than where you live. Write a message about its beauty and send it to someone.	**10** Compare and contrast the conservation of natural resources of any two parks on your list. Use a Venn diagram to show your findings.
11 Predict which state parks will be used by citizens of your community 100 years from now.	**12** Write a poem about conservation of natural resources at a specific park on your list. Generate a list of special words that convey ideas to help you with this task.	**13** Survey students in your class to determine which state park is most popular with them. Graph the results.	**14** Prepare a one- or two-minute commercial for a state park that you think families of your community would enjoy visiting.	**15** Create a bumper sticker to advertise a state park on your list.
16 Plan a perfect day for you and a group of friends to spend exploring one of the parks on your list.	**17** Research the history of one state park on your list to find out why the site was selected, how it was developed, and how well the conservation goals are being met.	**18** Make up an original game or plans for a recreational activity to be enjoyed in a specific park on your list.	**19** Name things that you hope will never happen to the natural resources of your favorite state park.	**20** Develop a script for a video presentation to summarize the effect that the laws and regulations of your state have on the role of the state parks in the conservation of natural resources.

Ocean Life
Making Waves

1 Examine a world map or globe to locate the major oceans of the world.	**2** List the oceans and give a brief description of the location of each.	**3** Name at least ten animals that live in the ocean.	**4** Select one ocean animal to research and write a brief report on it.	**5** Create a collage or series of pictures to show ocean animals that provide food for human beings.
6 The most feared of all sea animals is probably the shark. Find out why.	**7** Design a poster to tell swimmers and boaters how to protect themselves from sharks.	**8** Name some other sea animals that are dangerous to human beings and give their characteristics.	**9** Find out how deep-sea divers protect themselves from dangerous sea animals. Look at their training, protective clothing, and other precautions. Show your findings in a chart.	**10** The whale is a mammal with many unusual habits. Use research materials to learn about its lifestyle and distinguishing characteristics.
11 Find out why whales are in danger of becoming extinct and find out the steps that are being taken to protect them.	**12** Use a Venn diagram to show the similarities of and the differences between dolphins and porpoises.	**13** Research the grouper, the tuna, and the marlin. Find out in what parts of the world each can be found, and how each is caught and prepared.	**14** Draw an underwater scene showing a lobster, a jellyfish, and one other ocean animal, all protecting themselves from predators.	**15** Describe the barracuda. Explain why it has been portrayed in folklore and fiction as a fierce and highly aggressive animal.
16 The sea urchin, octopus, and triggerfish trap prey in unusual ways. Use research materials to find out how each does this, and give the names of the unfortunate prey.	**17** Name three underwater plants that are useful to human beings. Tell how they are harvested and what they are used for.	**18** Devise a brand-new recipe for preparing shrimp, scallops, or crab for a gala seafood dinner.	**19** Design a picture postcard. Write to a friend telling of a pretend vacation to a well-known beach. Identify and locate the ocean, and include a reference to the animals found there.	**20** List six or eight careers related to the animals living in the world's waterways and give a brief description of the requirements for each one.

Computers in the Classroom

1 Do some research to find out what the first computers were like. How does an early computer compare with the computer in your classroom?	**2** Find out how your school acquired the computer in your classroom.	**3** Make a list of any special features of your classroom computer (CD-ROM player, modem, scanner, etc.).	**4** Make a list of ways you can use a word processor in the classroom.	**5** What are the advantages of using a computer for creating a report or a piece of fiction when compared to writing by hand or typing?
6 What is a database?	**7** What is a spreadsheet?	**8** Create an original drawing based on your thoughts about or understanding of the "Information Superhighway."	**9** Come up with at least one new idea for using the computer to help with classroom learning. Submit your idea to your teacher.	**10** Write a brief paper to persuade the school board of the benefits of increasing funding for technology in the classroom.
11 Write a brief paper to persuade the school board that money spent on technology in the classroom would be better spent in other areas.	**12** Using the graphics program on the computer, create a logo for a Cooperative Learning group.	**13** Learn how to keep the computer's printer in good working order. Write a set of instructions for someone else to follow.	**14** Design a set of guidelines for students to follow when using the computer to prevent it from becoming dirty or damaged.	**15** Write an adventure story that features the concept of Virtual Reality.
16 Discover ways the computer can help you with projects for mathematics classes.	**17** Create a list of questions to ask adults about how their lives have been affected by computer technology. Conduct your survey. Present some of the results in graph form.	**18** Write a myth about a technology-based society that might be told by people in a society that lacked high technology.	**19** Prepare an explanation of how a computer works. Make it an explanation that could be given to a first-grader.	**20** Work as a class to create a presentation for the school on a favorite topic. Use the computer to create announcements, small posters, hall banners, and graphic reports.

Simple Machines

Six Simple Machines

1	2	3	4	5
Define machine.	Write the names of all the machines you can list in three minutes.	Design a classification system for your list of machines.	Do some research to learn about the first machines devised by humans.	List the six simple machines that are the basis of all machines, simple or complex.
6	7	8	9	10
Find out the level of efficiency of each of the six simple machines.	Create a crossword puzzle among whose words can be found the names of the six simple machines.	The wheel is often referred to in everyday speech, as in: "We don't need to invent the wheel all over again." Invent a new saying or metaphor that refers to one of the other simple machines.	Find out what a Rube Goldberg machine is. Make a drawing of a Rube Goldberg style machine. It can be humorous, but be sure to include forms of all six simple machines.	Define fulcrum.
11	12	13	14	15
What is the name of the force that prevents all machines from working at 100% efficiency?	Write an imaginary scenario about the discovery of one of the simple machines.	Find out what each of these parts for specialized machines does: ball bearing, gear, piston, V-belt pulley, universal joint, flexible shaft.	Invent a way to use a pulley to make classroom activities more convenient.	Think of a way an inclined plane could be used to make housework easier.
16	17	18	19	20
Write a poem or other original work praising (or deploring) the coming of the machine age.	How do machines reduce the amount of human effort required to perform work?	Make a list of questions you would like to ask an engineer who designs specialized machines.	Design a poster that could be used to teach a younger child about the six simple machines.	Pay close attention to your daily activities to see how you use the principles of simple machines in order to get your work done (and to play).

Using Integrated Instructional Strategies to Promote Cooperative Learning and Group Interaction

Using Cooperative Learning as an Instructional Tool

A cooperative learning group is an excellent means of teaching basic skills or reinforcing important concepts in any content area. Cooperative learning, as described by Johnson and Johnson (1991), involves teamwork within small groups of heterogeneous students working in a structured setting, with assigned roles, and towards a common goal. The five elements that distinguish cooperative learning from traditional group work, according to the Johnsons, are:

POSITIVE INTERDEPENDENCE
. . . requires the students to assist one another in the learning process through common goals, joint rewards, shared resources, and specified role assignments.

FACE-TO-FACE INTERACTION
. . . requires the students to actively engage in discussion, problem solving, decision making, and mutual assignment completion.

INDIVIDUAL ACCOUNTABILITY
. . . requires the student to carry through on "his or her share of the work" and to contribute as an individual to the established common goals.

INTERPERSONAL SKILLS
. . . require group members to learn and apply a range of communication and active learning skills.

GROUP PROCESSING
. . . requires the students to consistently evaluate their ability to function as a group by obtaining legitimate feedback and reinforcement.

Although roles for cooperative learning groups vary, the most common roles are those of Recorder, Time Keeper, Manager, Gopher, and Encourager.

Rules for cooperative learning groups vary too, but the most common are the following:

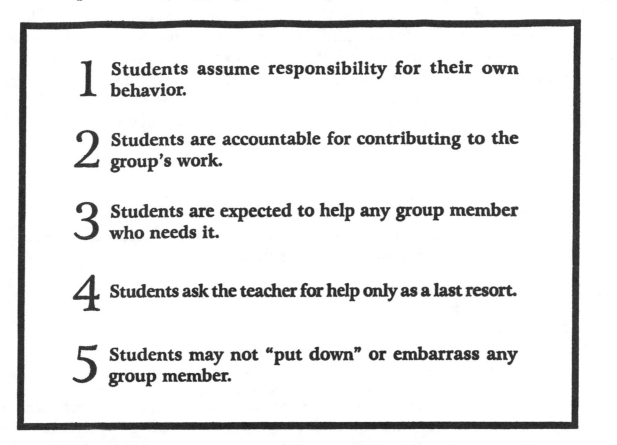

1 Students assume responsibility for their own behavior.

2 Students are accountable for contributing to the group's work.

3 Students are expected to help any group member who needs it.

4 Students ask the teacher for help only as a last resort.

5 Students may not "put down" or embarrass any group member.

The size of cooperative groups can range from pairs and trios to larger groups of four to six. It is important to keep in mind, however, that the smaller the group, the more chance there is for active participation and interaction of all group members. Groups of two, for example, can theoretically "have the floor" for fifty percent of the learning time, while groups of five can theoretically do so for only twenty percent of the learning time, if all are to contribute to the group goal in an equitable fashion. Likewise, it is important to note that groups should most often be put together in a random or arbitrary fashion so that the combination of group members varies with each task and so that group members represent a more heterogeneous type of placement. This can be done in a variety of ways ranging from "drawing names out of a hat" to having kids "count off" so those with the same numbers can be grouped together.

There are many different formats that can be used with cooperative learning groups and each of them has its advantages. On the following pages are descriptions to provide teachers with several structures that can be used in developing lesson plans around the cooperative learning method of instruction. Several applications for each of these structures can be found on pages 91 through 118.

THINK/PAIR/SHARE

In this format, the teacher gives the students a piece of information through a delivery system such as the lecturette, videotape, or transparency talk. The teacher then poses a higher-order question related to the information presented. Students are asked to reflect on the question and write down their responses after appropriate waiting time has passed. Students are then asked to turn to a partner and share responses. Teachers should prepare a plan ahead of time for ways in which students will be paired. If time allows, one pair of students may share ideas with another pair of students, making groups of four. Sufficient time for discussion and for all students to speak should be allowed. The advantages of this structure are:

- It is easy to use in large classes.

- It gives students time to reflect on course content.

- It allows students time to rehearse and embellish information before sharing with a small group or entire class.

- It fosters long-term retention of course content.

THREE-STEP INTERVIEW

In this format, the teacher presents students with information on a given topic or concept. The teacher then pairs students and asks a question about the information such as "What do you think about . . . ?" or "How would you describe . . . ?" or "Why is this important . . . ?" Each member of the pair responds to the question while the other practices active listening skills, knowing that he or she will have to speak for his or her partner at a later time. Each pair is then grouped with another pair so that each group member becomes one of four members. Person Two answers the question using the words of Person One and Person Three answers the questions using the words of Person Four. Roles are exchanged, and this process is repeated four times. The advantages of this structure are:

- It fosters important listening skills.

- It forces the student to articulate a position or response from another person's perspective.

- It presents multiple interpretations of the same information.

CIRCLE OF KNOWLEDGE

The teacher places students in groups of four to six. A Recorder (who does not participate in the brainstorming because he or she is busy writing down responses) is assigned to each group by the teacher. A question or prompt is given. Everyone takes a turn to brainstorm and respond to the question or prompt, beginning with the person to the left of the Recorder. Responses should be given by individuals around the circle, in sequence, as many times as possible within a five-minute period of time or "until the well runs dry." Group Recorders are asked to report responses from their group to the whole class without repeating an idea already shared by another group Recorder. These collective responses are written on the chalkboard or on a piece of chart paper for all to see.

- This structure is good for review and reinforcement of learned material or for introducing a new unit of study.

- It gives every student an equal opportunity to respond and participate.

- It lets a student know in advance when it is his or her turn to contribute.

- It does not judge the quality of a student's response.

- It fosters listening skills through the rule of "no repetition of the same or similar ideas in either the brainstorming or sharing processes."

TEAM LEARNING

In this cooperative learning format, the teacher places students in groups of four. Each group is given a Recording Sheet and asked to appoint a Recorder and to assign other group roles. The Recording Sheet is a "group worksheet" that contains four to six questions or tasks to be completed. A team must reach consensus on a group response for each question/task only after each member has provided input. The Recorder writes down the consensus response. When the work is finished, all team members review the group responses and sign the Recording Sheet to show they have read it, edited it, and agreed with it. These papers are collected and graded. The advantages of this structure are:

- Students build, criticize (positively), and edit one another's ideas.

- Teachers only have a few papers to grade since there is only one per group rather than one per student.

- Students collaborate on the work for a group grade rather than compete for an individual grade.

A wide variety of springboards can be used for Team Learning questions/tasks such as math manipulatives (tangrams, meter sticks, protractors), reading materials (poems, editorials, short stories), science tools (charts/graphs, rock collections, lab manuals), or social studies aids (globes, maps, compasses).

ROUND TABLE

In this cooperative learning format, the teacher forms groups of four to six members. The teacher gives each group of students a comprehensive problem to solve, an open-ended question to answer, or a complex activity to complete. Each student is asked to consider the assigned tasks and to record an individual response in writing. The key factor is that a group is given only one sheet of paper and one pencil. The sheet of paper is moved to the left around the group and, one at a time, each group member records his or her response on the sheet. No one is allowed to skip a turn. The students then determine an answer to represent the group's thinking, constructing a response that synthesizes many ideas. An optional final stage: each group shares its collective response with the whole class. The advantages of this structure are:

- It requires application of higher-order thinking skills.

- It is useful for reviewing material or practicing a skill.

- It fosters interdependence among group members.

JIGSAW

In this structure, the teacher forms home cooperative learning groups of six members and assigns each member a number from 1 to 6. Each member of a home group leaves that group to join another made up of one member of each of the other groups. The purpose of this arrangement is to have groups of students become experts on one aspect of a problem to be solved or a piece of information to be analyzed. In essence, Jigsaw is so named because it is a strategy in which each member of a given group gets only one piece of the information or problem-solving puzzle at a time. The teacher then presents each of the "expert groups" with a portion of a problem or one piece of an information paper to research, study, and acquire in-depth knowledge. Each "expert" member is responsible for mastering the content or concepts and developing a strategy for teaching it to the home team. The "expert" then returns to the home team and teaches all other members about his or her information or problem, and learns the information presented by the other group members as well. The advantages of this structure are:

- It fosters individual accountability through use of the "expert" role.

- It promotes group interdependence through "teaching and learning" processes.

- It encourages the use of high-quality communication skills through the teacher and learner roles.

Student Directions:
THINK/PAIR/SHARE

A **Think/Pair/Share** activity is designed to provide you and a partner with some "food for thought" on a given topic so that you can both write down your ideas and share your responses with each other. Follow these directions when completing the Recording Sheet.

1 Listen carefully to the information on the topic of the day presented by your teacher. Take notes on the important points.

2 Use the Recording Sheet to write down the assigned question or task as well as your response to that question or task.

3 Discuss your ideas with a partner and record something of interest he or she shared.

4 If time permits, you and your partner should share your combined ideas with another pair of students.

5 Determine why "two, three, or four heads are better than one."

A List of Possible
Think/Pair/Share
Springboards for Science

LIFE SCIENCE

1. Explain what is meant by life science.

2. What are some ways we measure size and shape?

3. Where do organisms get the things they need to stay alive?

4. Define a food chain and give an example of one.

5. How can we see a "zoo" in a tiny drop of water?

6. All living things perform life functions. Describe some of these functions.

7. Define what is meant by a scientific theory and give an example to illustrate your definition.

8. Describe the importance of the cell to living things.

9. Explain why scientists group living things into classification systems.

10. Summarize the functions of the roots, stems, and leaves of a plant.

11. How would you tell the differences in flatworms, roundworms, and segmented worms?

12. Describe the major characteristics of cells.

13. Explain how you would test for sugar, starch, proteins, and fats in food.

14. Discuss how living things get energy.

15. Summarize ways you can help your body work properly.

16. Which body system do you think is most interesting? Most intricate? Most important? Most difficult to understand?

17. Explain how the eye or ear works.

18. What is a habit? How is a habit formed?

19. How do we learn?

20. How can our senses fool us?

21. Explain why there are times when bacteria can be helpful and times when they can be harmful.

22. Discuss how the body defends itself against disease.

23. Describe how one can practice preventive medicine.

24. Explain where you think living things come from.

25. Discuss how offspring can look different from parents.

26. How do you feel about the emerging science of genetic engineering?

27. Explain what is meant by an ecosystem.

28. What are the differences in a food chain, a web, and a pyramid?

29. Do you feel that you are in balance with your environment? Why or why not?

30. Discuss the careers in science you would or would not like to have.

31. You are a red blood cell. Describe your round trip through the circulatory system.

32. You are a hamburger. Describe your trip through the digestive system.

33. Discuss the advantages and disadvantages of being a vegetarian.

34. Describe the ecosystem of the rain forest.

35. Why are rain forests sometimes referred to as the "lungs" of the planet?

EARTH SCIENCE

1. Explain how a scientist goes about studying the earth.

2. What do you think the inside of the earth looks like?

3. Describe ways you could identify various minerals.

4. What are some of your favorite gems or precious stones, and what makes them valuable to you and others?

5. Explain how you might tell an igneous rock from a metamorphic rock, and both from a sedimentary rock.

6. What is the difference between mechanical weathering and chemical weathering?

7. Describe some forms of life that one might find in the soil.

8. Give some examples of different types of erosion, how erosion occurs, and what can be done to prevent it under different circumstances.

9. Discuss some ways you can learn about the earth's past.

10. Describe some things that fascinate you about the ocean.

©1996 by Incentive Publications, Inc., Nashville, TN.

11. What do you think it would be like to live in an underwater city?

12. Discuss ways we can identify various cloud formations.

13. How has your lifestyle contributed to the pollution of the water, earth, and sky?

14. Describe some of the factors that determine climate.

15. What do people find fascinating about the stars, the planets, and other bodies in outer space?

16. Discuss some special features of the sun.

17. Describe some of your beliefs about life on other planets.

18. How do you feel about UFO sightings? Do you think they are sightings of real space travelers?

19. What do you think life is like for astronauts?

20. Explain what makes day and night.

21. Discuss ways that we measure time.

22. What are some ways to tell the ages of things such as rocks, glaciers, and fossils?

23. What do we mean when we refer to the earth's resources?

24. Discuss why people collect rocks.

25. Owning a pet rock was a popular fad with kids several years ago. Can you explain the appeal of such a pet?

26. Brainstorm a list of jobs or careers related to the earth sciences. Which ones appeal to you?

PHYSICAL SCIENCE

1. Describe the different forms of energy.

2. What is work? How would it be defined by a scientist, a doctor, a teacher, and a politician?

3. Discuss ways that machines help us at home and at school.

4. Why do things fall?

5. Who was Newton and what did he accomplish?

6. Is friction good or bad?

7. How would you define temperature?

8. What is sound?

9. What is music?

10. Discuss various musical instruments and how they work.

11. Explain how light originates.

12. What is the secret of the camera lens?

13. Describe how we see.

14. Summarize the method for setting up an electric circuit. How does it differ from a parallel circuit?

15. Explain how the earth is like a magnet.

16. Generate a working definition of matter.

Recording Sheet

Science

NAME_____

DATE_____

QUESTION OR TASK TO BE COMPLETED: _____

_____
_____
_____
_____
_____
_____
_____
_____

MY IDEAS ON THE TOPIC: _____

_____
_____
_____
_____
_____
_____
_____
_____
_____
_____
_____

IDEAS SHARED BY MY PARTNER(S): _____

_____
_____
_____
_____
_____
_____
_____
_____
_____
_____
_____

Student Directions:
THREE-STEP INTERVIEW

In the **Three-Step Interview** activity, you will be given some information on a topic by your teacher, then you will work with a partner to discuss your ideas on the topic. You and your partner must take turns as active listener and as active speaker. Follow these directions in completing the Recording Sheet.

1 Work with an assigned partner and decide who will be the first speaker and who will be the first listener.

2 Read the information on "Gun Control" given to you by your teacher. Think carefully about the information.

3 Use the Recording Sheet to prepare your written responses to the five questions. You will use these responses as a basis for discussing the subject with your partner.

4 After talking to your partner while he or she carefully listens to your ideas, exchange roles and let your partner give responses while you listen intently. You may want to take some notes about what he or she tells you.

5 As time permits, you and your partner are to join another pair of students and share opinions and information about gun control.

Background Information

The World of Matter

Matter is anything that takes up space. It can be a speck of sand or a drop of water or a forest of trees or a river of fish. Matter comes in three different forms, called states, which are solids, liquids, and gases. A solid has a definite shape, mass, and volume. A liquid has mass and volume but takes the shape of its container. A gas has mass, but has no specific volume (or shape). It expands to fill its container regardless of the container's shape or volume.

Chemistry is the study of matter. Chemists study the characteristics of matter and the way different kinds of matter behave or react to a wide variety of conditions.

Matter is described in two major ways. It has **physical properties,** which are things we can see or feel but that don't affect the way material reacts. It also has **chemical properties,** which do affect the way a substance reacts. A block of wood, for example, has physical properties of size, weight, and a particular appearance. When the block of wood is burned in a fire, however, it changes to something else, such as ash, soot, gas, and heat, demonstrating its chemical properties.

Matter can be grouped in categories based on physical and chemical properties. The categories include **acids, bases, metals,** and **nonmetals.**

Recording Sheet, Page 1   NAME_____

The World of Matter   DATE_____

Use the background information on the world of matter to answer these questions and to share with your partner. Be sure to record some of your partner's ideas from the sharing session as well as your own.

1. Make a list of at least five different solids, liquids, and gases.

YOUR THOUGHTS:

_____
_____
_____
_____
_____

YOUR PARTNER'S THOUGHTS:

_____
_____
_____
_____
_____

2. Select one of your solids, liquids, and gases from the chart. Describe its physical and chemical properties.

YOUR THOUGHTS:

_____
_____
_____
_____

YOUR PARTNER'S THOUGHTS:

_____
_____
_____
_____
_____

Recording Sheet, Page 2

The World of Matter

3. Give an example of a common household solution, heterogeneous mixture, homogeneous mixture.

YOUR THOUGHTS:

_____
_____
_____
_____
_____

YOUR PARTNER'S THOUGHTS:

_____
_____
_____
_____
_____
_____

4. Explain how H_2O can be a solid, liquid, and gas. How do its states of matter change?

YOUR THOUGHTS:

_____
_____
_____
_____
_____

YOUR PARTNER'S THOUGHTS:

_____
_____
_____
_____
_____
_____

Recording Sheet, Page 3

The World of Matter

5. Give three reasons that you would or would not like to be a chemist.

YOUR THOUGHTS:

_____
_____
_____
_____
_____

YOUR PARTNER'S THOUGHTS:

_____
_____
_____
_____
_____
_____

6. Are you more like a solid, a liquid, or a gas? Explain.

YOUR THOUGHTS:

_____
_____
_____
_____

YOUR PARTNER'S THOUGHTS:

_____
_____
_____
_____
_____

Student Directions:
CIRCLE OF KNOWLEDGE

A Circle of Knowledge activity provides a small group situation for brainstorming responses to a given question or prompt presented by the teacher. Follow these directions in completing the Recording Sheet.

1 Agree on a Recorder for your group. Direct the Recorder to write down the names of all group members and the assigned question or prompt in the appropriate sections of the Recording Sheet.

2 Share your responses to the question or prompt when it is your turn in the circle. Make sure you are ready to respond and that your ideas are recorded as given by the Recorder.

3 Assist the Recorder during the large-group sharing of all responses by helping him or her note which ideas have already been given by the other groups in the class and therefore should not be repeated when it is your group's turn to share.

4 Review the responses generated by both your group and the large group that have been recorded on the chalkboard, transparency, or chart paper.

5 Determine why "two, three, or four heads are better than one."

Recording Sheet

DATE_____

Circle of Knowledge

GROUP MEMBERS:

1. _____
2. _____
3. _____
4. _____
5. _____
6. _____

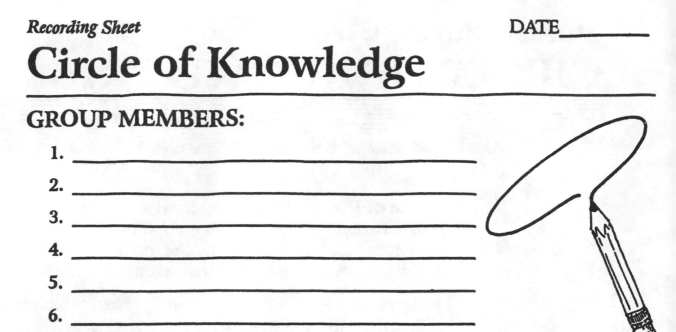

QUESTION OR PROMPT FOR BRAINSTORMING:

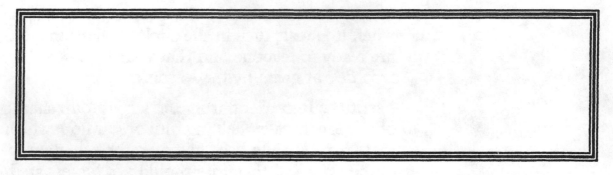

COLLECTIVE RESPONSES:

Sample Questions or Prompts for Circle of Knowledge Activities

LIFE SCIENCE

1. Name a tool of a scientist and explain how it is used.

2. Give an example of a vertebrate (or invertebrate) animal.

3. Cite an example of a type of food chain.

4. Cite an example of a type of cycle.

5. List the systems (or organs within systems) of the human body and tell the primary function of each.

6. Give as many uses for plants as you can.

7. Give an example of a predator-prey situation.

8. Make a list of as many careers as you can think of that are related to life science.

9. Give examples of nonvascular plants.

10. Give examples of vascular plants with (or without) seeds.

11. Name nutrients important to plant (or human) life.

12. List substances that can be harmful to the body.

13. State as many facts as you can about the human body.

14. State as many facts as you can about plants.

PHYSICAL SCIENCE

1. List the elements of the periodic table with their correct symbols.

2. Name acids (or bases).

3. List compounds and their formulas.

4. Cite alternative forms of energy.

5. List conductors of electricity.

6. Think of insulators of electricity.

7. Think of items that would be attracted to a magnet.

8. Name simple (or compound) machines.

9. Describe ways machines help us work.

10. List as many ways as you can think of that chemistry is practiced in the home.

11. Name as many careers related to physical science as you can.

12. List as many reasons for an energy crisis as you can.

13. Cite as many results as you can that would come from turning off electricity in a community for a month.

14. List as many facts related to your study of magnetism as you can.

15. List as many uses of thermonuclear energy as you can.

16. List as many forms of energy as you can.

EARTH SCIENCE

1. List as many facts about the solar system as you can.

2. Name and define weather words.

3. Cite as many precious gems as you can recall.

4. List important minerals that have nonmetallic luster.

5. Name the gases of the earth's atmosphere and tell something about each one.

6. List the causes of different weather conditions.

7. List as many facts about the ocean as you can.

8. Give as many causes of erosion as you can.

9. List natural disasters.

10. List as many different landforms as you can.

11. Name as many careers related to earth science as you can.

12. Give reasons people might want to travel in outer space.

13. Name the earth's multiple resources.

14. Distinguish between renewable and nonrenewable resources.

15. List distinguishing elements of each of the four seasons.

Student Directions:
TEAM LEARNING

During a **Team Learning** activity, your cooperative learning group will respond collectively to questions and tasks. Assign the role of Recorder to one member of your group. The Recorder should follow these directions to complete the Recording Sheet:

1 Assign one of the following jobs to each member of your group so that each person has at least one job: Timekeeper, Coordinator, Checker, and Evaluator (some members may have more than one task to perform).

2 Distribute a copy of the Recording Sheet to each group member. Ask all to read the questions and tasks.

3 Discuss your ideas for each item and reach consensus on a group response for each item. The Recorder is to write down these collaborative responses to questions and tasks. The Coordinator is to facilitate the discussion. The Timekeeper is to keep track of the time allotted for the assignment. The Checker is to read through the responses orally, checking for grammar, comprehension, and consensus errors.

4 All cooperative learning group members are to sign their names at the bottom of the Recording Sheet, indicating agreement with the responses and acknowledging fair contributions to the work.

108

DATE_____

Conservation Begins at Home

TEAM MEMBERS:

1. _____
2. _____
3. _____
4. _____
5. _____
6. _____

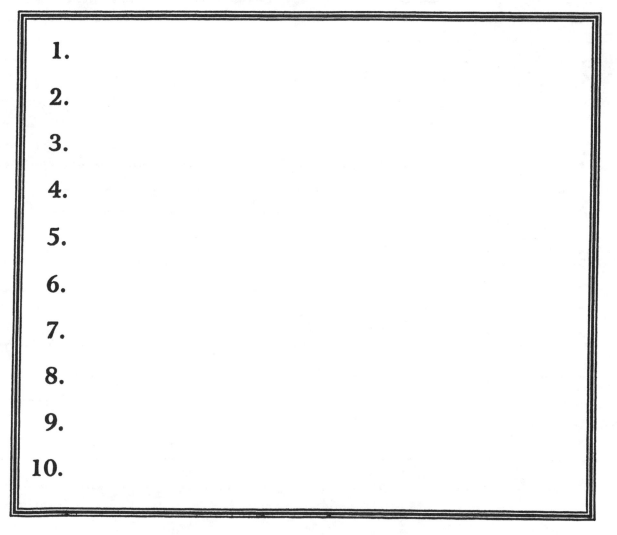

List ten things that you see students do at home, at school, or in the community that contribute to a waste of natural resources.

1.

2.

3.

4.

5.

6.

7.

8.

9.

10.

Recording Sheet, Page 2

Conservation Begins at Home

Analyze these conservation statistics and respond to each.

STAT ONE: Every day American families produce an estimated four million pounds of dangerous household wastes such as paints and batteries.

_____

_____

STAT TWO: Americans use more energy than they produce.

_____

_____

_____

STAT THREE: Paper makes up about 41% of the trash in the United States.

_____

_____

_____

Write down five ways you and your friends or family could reuse resources (such as glass bottles, shopping bags, etc.) without sending them to a recycling center.

1. _____

_____

2. _____

_____

3. _____

_____

4. _____

_____

5. _____

_____

Signatures:

_____   _____

_____   _____

_____   _____

Student Directions:
ROUND TABLE

During the **Round Table** activity, you and your assigned group will criticize science entries about LIGHT from at least three different encyclopedia sources by recording individual responses to a set of questions "round robin" style. Some LIGHT topics to consider are REFLECTION, REFRACTION, SPEED OF LIGHT, SPECTRUM, PRISMS, and MIRAGES. It is important that you read about the same topic from each of the encyclopedia sources so that you can compare and contrast the quality of information reported in each encyclopedia. Follow these directions when completing the Recording Sheets (there will be three sets of each recording sheet).

1 Decide on the order for recording responses. Who will go first, second, third, fourth, fifth, and sixth?

2 Use the Recording Sheets to write everybody's responses to both questions. After the first person writes down his or her idea, the paper is moved to the left around the group. No one may skip a turn.

3 The paper should be passed around the group twice, making certain that each member of the group responds to Question 1 only on the first round and Question 2 only on the second round.

4 One person in the group is responsible for completing information at the top of the Recording Sheet.

5 After both questions have been answered by all six members, the group should analyze the responses and synthesize the ideas represented for each question into a comprehensive paragraph.

Recording Sheet, Page 1

DATE_____

Light

GROUP MEMBERS:

1. _____
2. _____
3. _____
4. _____
5. _____
6. _____

TITLE OF ENCYCLOPEDIA: _____

PUBLISHER: _____

TITLE OF SELECTION: _____

PAGE NUMBER: _____

STUDENT ONE RESPONSE

Question 1: What was the main idea of this encyclopedia selection?

STUDENT TWO RESPONSE

Question 1: What was the main idea of this encyclopedia selection?

Recording Sheet, Page 2

STUDENT THREE RESPONSE

Question 1: What was the main idea of this encyclopedia selection?

STUDENT FOUR RESPONSE

Question 1: What was the main idea of this encyclopedia selection?

STUDENT FIVE RESPONSE

Question 1: What was the main idea of this encyclopedia selection?

STUDENT SIX RESPONSE

Question 1: What was the main idea of this encyclopedia selection?

Recording Sheet, Page 3
STUDENT ONE RESPONSE

Question 2: Which fact did I find to be most interesting?

STUDENT TWO RESPONSE

Question 2: Which fact did I find to be most interesting?

STUDENT THREE RESPONSE

Question 2: Which fact did I find to be most interesting?

Recording Sheet, Page 4
STUDENT FOUR RESPONSE

Question 2: Which fact did I find to be most interesting?

STUDENT FIVE RESPONSE

Question 2: Which fact did I find to be most interesting?

STUDENT SIX RESPONSE

Question 2: Which fact did I find to be most interesting?

Student Directions:
JIGSAW ACTIVITY

During the **Jigsaw** activity you will work in a group of six in order to learn something new about invertebrate animals, and then teach this information to members of your home group. Follow these directions in order to complete the Recording Sheet.

1 Assign a number from one through six to each member of your home group.

2 With the help of your teacher, give each member of your group his or her appropriately numbered paragraph describing some important aspect of invertebrate animals. Don't let anyone see any paragraph but his or her own.

3 When the teacher gives you the signal, locate the other people in small home groups in your classroom who have a number the same as yours. Meet with them and together learn the information discussed in your paragraph so that each of you becomes an "expert" on its content. Once you have learned this information, have the group decide on a strategy for teaching it to the other members of your home group.

4 Return to your home team and teach all of the other members about your paragraph. Learn the information presented by them in their assigned paragraphs as well.

Recording Sheets

Invertebrate Animals

HOME GROUP MEMBERS:

STUDENT **1** _____

STUDENT **2** _____

STUDENT **3** _____

STUDENT **4** _____

STUDENT **5** _____

STUDENT **6** _____

Cut apart the paragraphs about invertebrate animals. Give each section to the appropriate person in your group. Meet with the other students in the class who have numbers the same as yours and learn the information discussed in the paragraph.

STUDENT **1** Sponges (Porifera)

Sponges are the simplest of many-celled animals. They come in a variety of colors, make their home on the ocean floor, and attach themselves to rocks for survival. The basic shape of a sponge is like that of a vase with a wide opening at the top. The sponge's body is actually a food-gathering tube. As water passes through the sponge, special cells trap and digest tiny food particles. Other cells pass the wastes back into the water.

STUDENT **2** Stinging-cell Animals (Coelenterates)

Coelenterates include jellyfish, corals, and hydras. Each has a tube-shaped or an umbrella-shaped body with an opening or mouth that is surrounded by tentacles. The body of a coelenterate is made of three layers and its cells are organized into tissues. The tentacles contain special stinging cells that are used to immobilize prey. Hydras live in lakes and ponds, while the other coelenterates live in the ocean.

STUDENT 3 Mollusks (Mollusca)

The three major classes of mollusk live in salt water, in fresh water, and on land. One class consists of mollusks with two-part shells such as clams, oysters, and mussels. The second class includes mollusks with one shell, such as snails, and the third class, with little or no shell, includes squids and octopuses. Mollusks have three parts: a head with a mouth, sense organs, and a brain; a body; and a "foot" for creeping.

STUDENT 4 Arthropods (Arthropoda)

The word "arthropod" comes from a Greek word meaning "jointed foot." Arthropods have exoskeletons made of chitin (a hard, chalky substance), jointed limbs, and hairs or bristles that act as sense organs. Arthropods are found from the bottom of the ocean to mountain heights. Depending on where they live, how they move, and what they eat, different kinds of arthropods have different body structures. Lobsters and crabs have large claws for getting food. Insects have special mouth parts that are used for chewing or for sucking, and most have wings.

STUDENT 5 Flatworms, Roundworms, and Segmented Worms
(Platyhelminthes, Nematoda, and Annelida)

A flatworm has a body that is flattened, like a ribbon, and a head and simple nervous system. It lives in water or moist places. Three varieties are planaria, flukes, and tapeworms. Flukes and tapeworms are parasites that live inside other organisms. Roundworms are round, threadlike worms that can live anywhere, although most live in water or the soil. Roundworms, though simple animals, have complete digestive systems. Segmented worms, including leeches and earthworms, have digestive systems, developed circulatory and nervous systems, many body sections, and true sense organs.

STUDENT 6 Sea Stars and Their Relatives (Echinoderms)

Echinoderms, such as the starfish, sand dollar, sea urchin, and sea cucumber, are spiny-skinned animals that live on the sandy bottom of the ocean. An echinoderm has hard, spiny skin and body structures arranged like the spokes of a wheel around a central body point. It moves using small sucker-like structures called tube feet that work like a water-pumping system to pull the animal forward.

Using Integrated Instructional Strategies to Facilitate Authentic Assessment

An Overview of Authentic Assessment

In comparison with traditional types of assessment, assessment practices today emphasize more authentic ways to demonstrate that student learning has taken place. There is less assessment of the recall of information and more of the processing of information. Collecting evidence about a student over time in realistic settings is the best way to document growth and acquisition of both skills and content.

Product, performance, and portfolio assessment offer alternative assessment methods. They are all more authentic than traditional methods because they:

- require collaboration among student, teacher, and peers;
- encourage student ownership through self-assessment;
- set flexible time limits;
- are scored through multi-faceted systems;
- allow for student strengths and weaknesses;
- make use of individual learning styles and interests; and
- minimize competition.

In short, authentic assessment is designed to reflect real-world applications of knowledge whenever possible.

PRODUCT ASSESSMENT
. . . requires the student to produce a concrete end result. This can take many forms, ranging from a videotape or experiment to an exhibit or report.

PERFORMANCE ASSESSMENT
. . . requires the student to actively demonstrate a set of skills and processes while performing a predetermined task.

PORTFOLIO ASSESSMENT
. . . requires the student to maintain a collection of artifacts that reflects the student's overall efforts, progress, and achievements in one or more areas. It is important to note that both products and performances can and should become artifacts contained within the portfolio itself.

Assessment is also made more authentic through the consistent use of rubrics and metacognitive reflections throughout the assessment experience.

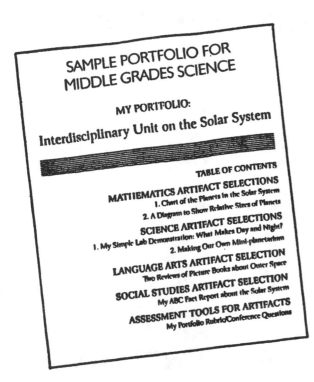

Rubrics are checklists that contain sets of criteria for measuring the elements of a product, performance, or portfolio. They can be designed as a qualitative measure (holistic rubric) to gauge overall performance to a prompt, or they can be designed as a quantitative measure (analytic rubric) to award points for each of several elements in a response to a prompt.

Metacognitive reflections are self-assessment observations and statements made by the individual student about each product or performance that he or she has completed. These reflections become part of the portfolio contents.

Although authentic assessment is designed to enhance and support the curriculum rather than dictate or limit the curriculum, it should be noted that more traditional types of measurements such as paper/pencil quizzes, objective end-of-chapter tests, and standardized achievement exams continue to play an important role in today's assessment practices. They should become one type of artifact included in the portfolio or one type of grade assigned to a performance or one type of measure used to determine the value of a product.

The following pages of this section provide the reader with a sample portfolio in science for a typical middle level student. This prototype is intended to show how authentic assessment—in the form of product, performance, and portfolio samples—can be used effectively to document student growth and achievement over time. It also contains student reflections and self-assessments that are intended to realistically appraise how the student is doing based on his or her own judgment in collaboration with the judgment of others, including the teacher.

Springboards for Journal Writing

REFLECTION STARTER STATEMENTS

1. Something important I learned from today's lesson is . . .
2. A question I have from today's discussion is . . .
3. I would like to know more about . . .
4. An idea from the textbook that puzzles me is . . .
5. I wish I didn't have to remember so much about . . . because . . .
6. I wonder if . . .
7. When I think about the videotape (book, movie), I am surprised that . . .
8. A concept I would like more information on is . . .
9. Some new terms I need to remember are . . .
10. The steps I followed in solving my problem (or completing my assignment) were . . .

SPRINGBOARDS FOR CRITICAL THINKING

1. **HOW ABOUT . . .**

   How about finding out why gems are precious?

   How about telling us why stars look blue?

2. **WHAT IF . . .**

   What if humans could camouflage themselves as animals do?

   What if there was life in parts of the universe other than our solar system?

3. **CAN YOU . . .**

   Can you write five sentences describing today's weather conditions?

   Can you make a list of supplies an astronaut might take on a space flight?

4. **WHAT ARE YOUR FEELINGS ABOUT . . .**

   What are your feelings about people who litter, adding to environmental pollution?

   What are your feelings about what it would be like to train as an astronaut?

5. **IN WHAT WAYS . . .**

   In what ways is space exploration like underwater exploration?

   In what ways are a telescope and a microscope alike?

SPRINGBOARDS FOR CREATIVE THINKING

1. **YOU ARE AN ADVISOR.**

   What advice would you give the director of the space program?

   What advice would you give someone who is training to be a weather forecaster or meteorologist?

2. **YOU ARE AN IMPROVER.**

   How would you make a space shuttle more comfortable?

   How would you improve a hammer, screwdriver, or a saw?

3. **YOU ARE A DESIGNER.**

   Design a new thermometer that does more than measure temperature.

   Design a new universal symbol for planet Earth.

4. **YOU ARE A WORD SPECIALIST.**

   Make a list of all the words you can think of that describe chemical changes.

   List the words you can make from the letters in the word PHOTOSYNTHESIS.

5. **YOU ARE A PROBLEM SOLVER.**

   What would you do if the taxpayers voted to eliminate the space program because of its costs?

   What would you do if you saw someone cheating on a science test?

6. **YOU ARE AN OBSERVER.**

   You are one of the first passengers on a space flight to the moon. Tell about it.

   You are one of the environmentalists reporting to the Department of the Interior. What would you say?

7. **YOU ARE A WRITER.**

   Write a letter to Ben Franklin warning him of the dangers of doing experiments such as he did with a key and a kite.

   Write a thank-you note to Georg Ohm telling him how much you appreciate his contribution to science through the creation of Ohm's Law.

8. **YOU ARE AN IDEA PERSON.**

   Think of ten different uses for a prism.

   Think of twenty ways to promote conservation among students and parents in your school and community.

SPRINGBOARDS BASED ON BLOOM'S TAXONOMY ≡

KNOWLEDGE LEVEL JOURNAL ENTRIES

a.   Record the contribution of each of the following scientists to the study of magnetism: William Gilbert, Hans Christian Oersted, and Michael Faraday.

b.   Locate and define five to ten important terms that are associated with light and sound.

COMPREHENSION LEVEL JOURNAL ENTRIES

a.   Summarize what you know about clouds.

b.   Give examples of how different animals reproduce.

APPLICATION LEVEL JOURNAL ENTRIES

a.   Discuss reasons different animal species are becoming endangered and/or extinct, and think of some things that can be done to slow this trend.

b.   Organize a panel discussion on a science topic of your choice. Make a list of important ideas to include in this discussion.

ANALYSIS LEVEL JOURNAL ENTRIES

a.   Debate the pros and cons of conducting research in genetic engineering. Try to list at least three pros and three cons when preparing for this debate.

b.   Survey members of your class or school to determine their perceptions of global warming and the greenhouse effect.

SYNTHESIS LEVEL JOURNAL ENTRIES

a.   Invent a new constellation for the night sky. Draw and describe it.

b.   Imagine you have designed a new machine that makes use of the wedge, lever, pulley, wheel, and inclined plane. Create an advertisement telling the world about it.

EVALUATION LEVEL JOURNAL ENTRIES

a.   Determine science topics that are the most difficult for you to learn. Give reasons for your answer.

b.   Rank the systems of the body first according to complexity, and then according to importance of function.

Springboards for Student Products

1. Prepare a set of Fact Cards about the important plants or animals that you have studied. On one side of the card, write down the vital statistics (size, species, classification, etc.) about the animal and on the other side of the card write down interesting information about its habits and habitats.

2. Draw a set of diagrams illustrating various formula masses of molecules. Do this:

    - **Write down the formula of the compound.**

    - **Find the atomic mass of each element in the compound. Use the periodic table.**

    - **Multiply the atomic mass of each element by its subscript. The subscript shows how many atoms of the element are in a molecule. If there is no subscript, that means there is only one atom of the element.**

    - **Add the total masses of all of the elements in the compound. That will give you the formula mass.**

3. Create a series of commemorative stamps or plates to honor the scientists of the world, past and present. Use these to set up a classroom Scientist Hall of Fame.

4. Plan and design a series of shadow boxes to show the different biomes of grasslands, deserts, scrublands, tundra, deciduous forests, coniferous forests, and tropical rain forests.

5. Construct a scale model of one of the following landforms:

    - mountains
    - caves
    - glaciers
    - caverns
    - volcanoes
    - canyons

6. Pretend you are the author of a new reference book about a science topic such as astronomy, invertebrates, or simple machines. Design a book cover for your publication that includes information about your topic, yourself, and the contents of your book.

7. Design a learning center for younger students on a science topic of your choice. Include a set of directions for completing the center, a set of task or activity cards, and a simple quiz.

8. Prepare a scroll showing the five kingdoms of living things:

   • ANIMALS

   • PLANTS

   • FUNGI

   • PROTISTS

   • MONERANS

9. Construct a project cube that describes and illustrates the water cycle or the rock cycle.

10. Make up a series of conversations between the various parts or systems of the body. Write these in cartoon and/or comic strip form.

11. Write directions and steps used in an experiment (complete with illustrations) so that someone else can do it.

12. Design a pictionary, jeopardy, or trivial pursuit game on a science topic of your choice.

13. Paint a mural showing the formation of igneous, sedimentary, and metamorphic rocks.

14. Draw a series of pictures showing various objects under the microscope. Make these into a puzzle or quiz and see if others can guess what is being depicted in each picture.

15. Pretend you are able to enter a space shuttle. Describe what you can see, hear, smell, and touch.

Springboards for Performances

1. Plan and participate in a panel discussion or a debate about a science topic of interest to you. Consider such controversial issues as:
   - genetic engineering
   - test tube babies
   - determining the gender of children
   - right to die in terminal cases
   - organ donors and transplants
   - prolonging life under any conditions
   - slowing the aging process

2. Prepare a series of radio or television commercials about one of the following environmental issues:
   - noise pollution
   - household dumping of toxic wastes
   - litter and graffiti

3. Prepare a set of verbal explanations for several different scientific theories such as the Big Bang Theory or the Theory of Relativity. Make these informative, clear, and as concise as you can to convey the ideas to others.

4. Pretend you have been selected to be an astronaut after a very thorough screening of potential candidates. Prepare an acceptance speech to share your thoughts and feelings at this time.

5. Create and act out a play in which the characters are elements of the periodic table or are the different states of matter.

6. Stage a drama to show the rotation of the planets with members of the class acting as the solar system.

7. Reenact great moments in science history. Consider moments such as:
   - first landing on the moon
   - discovering the vaccine for polio
   - finding a cure for yellow fever

8. Find ways to role play one of the following:
   • different ecosystems
   • different food chains or food webs
   • different cycles such as the water cycle or carbon/oxygen cycle

9. Plan a series of demonstrations to show how to use and care for the tools of the scientist. Consider:
   • the microscope
   • the balance scale
   • the spectroscope

10. Prepare a recording of sounds of things in the natural world (nature sounds) and narrate the recording with personal comments, anecdotes, and explanations.

11. Prepare and conduct a scientific experiment or investigation that requires you to perform the steps and activities before an audience.

12. Prepare and deliver a series of weather forecasts for your area over an extended period of time. Develop and use a set of visual props in your presentation.

13. Make up and perform a dance or exercise routine that demonstrates a scientific process such as erosion or plate tectonics.

14. Plan and conduct drill exercises on science content with a small group of students to prepare for an upcoming science quiz or test.

15. Organize a human graph to see where classmates stand on current science issues, trends, or paradigm shifts.

SAMPLE PORTFOLIO FOR MIDDLE GRADES SCIENCE

MY PORTFOLIO:

Interdisciplinary Unit on the Solar System

The Solar System

Chart of the Planets

PURPOSE

It is helpful to organize information about the planets in a way that makes it easy to quickly review facts about them. A chart is often the best way to do this. The chart on the next page shows key ideas to learn about the planets of the solar system.

WHAT I DID

I researched each of the nine planets of the solar system to find answers to the following questions:

1. What is the planet made of?

2. Does it have rings?

3. How many miles is this planet from the sun?

4. How many moons does it have?

5. What is the diameter of this planet?

6. How long is its year in Earth time?

7. How long is its day in Earth time?

8. What is its atmosphere like?

9. What is its temperature?

10. On this planet, what is the weight of an object that would weigh 100 pounds on Earth?

Wherever possible, I compared weights and measurements of the planets to those of things on Earth.

Next, I organized my data into a chart, arranging the planets in order according to distance in miles from the sun. I constructed my chart on a large piece of mural paper that I got from the art teacher. My teacher displayed my chart on the wall outside our classroom door because it was too big for the bulletin board.

Reflection:

I worked with two friends on this project to do the research. We each wrote our ideas on file cards, using one card for each planet. We compared cards to be sure we had all the information. I made my own chart. I could work out in the hall since it was too crowded to make the chart in the room. My chart looks good and it helps me remember stuff for the test.

CHART OF THE PLANETS

	MERCURY	VENUS	EARTH	MARS	JUPITER	SATURN	URANUS	NEPTUNE	PLUTO
MADE OF	Rock	Rock	Rock	Rock	Liquid & Gas	Liquid & Gas	Rock	Frozen Gas	Rock & Ice
RINGS	No	No	No	No	Yes	Yes	Yes	Yes	No
DISTANCE FROM SUN (MILES)	36 million	67 million	93 million	142 million	484 million	888 million	1.8 billion	2.8 billion	3.7 billion
MOONS	0	0	1	2	16	more than 20	15	8	1
DIAMETER (MILES)	3,030	7,565	7,973	4,243	88,700	75,105	32,500	30,700	1420
LENGTH OF YEAR (IN EARTH TIME)	88 days	227 days	365 days	687 days	11.9 years	29.5 years	84 years	165 years	248 years
LENGTH OF DAY (IN EARTH TIME)	58.7 days	243 days	24 hours	24.6 hours	9.9 hours	10.6 hours	17 1/4 hours	16 hours	6.4 days
ATMOSPHERE	Sodium, helium, hydrogen, oxygen	Carbon dioxide, nitrogen	nitrogen, oxygen, water	Carbon dioxide, nitrogen, argon	Hydrogen, helium	Hydrogen, helium	Hydrogen, helium	Hydrogen, helium, methane	Methane
TEMPERATURE	-180°C to 430°C	460°C	150°C	+24°C to -31°C	-149°C	-176°C	-218°C	-218°C	-208°C to -223°C
WEIGHT (OF OBJECT 100 POUNDS ON EARTH)	35 pounds	88 pounds	100 pounds	37 pounds	287 pounds	132 pounds	93 pounds	123 pounds	3 pounds

My Simple Lab Demonstration

What Makes Day and Night?

PURPOSE

It is important to understand that it is the rotation of the earth and not the movement of the sun that causes day and night. This concept can be demonstrated with simple tools and techniques.

WHAT I DID

I gathered together a globe, a base light, a piece of paper, and tape. I darkened the room and shined the base lamp on the globe. The lamp represented the sun and the globe represented Earth. I then cut a piece of paper and taped it on the globe to represent the city in which we live. Next, I rotated the globe to show what happens to our city as Earth rotates. Finally, I led a small group discussion to answer these questions:

1 How long does it take for Earth to rotate once?

2 Does Earth rotate from east to west or west to east?

3 Why are days longer than nights and nights longer than days at different times during the year?

4 What is the international date line?

A drawing of my demonstration is included in my portfolio file box.

Reflection:

Although this was a simple experiment, it did demonstrate rotation and it stimulated much class discussion. I think it is easier to understand new concepts if you can actually see them rather than just read about them. The kids in my small cooperative learning group enjoyed my presentation.

Drawing

What Makes Day and Night?

Making Our Own
Mini-planetarium

PURPOSE

After visiting the local planetarium in our community, we made our own "star show" by constructing constellations from tin cans. Each small group of students created a different set of star patterns and we shared these with the whole class.

WHAT I DID

Using a flashlight, a nail, a tin can, and a hammer, I made a great device for viewing constellations. Using the nail (and sometimes a punch), I made replicas of three different star patterns: Ursa Major (Big Bear), Orion (The Hunter), and Ursa Minor (Little Dipper).

Next, I darkened the room and inserted a lighted flashlight into the tin can so that the light would shine through the punched holes. I could observe star images produced on the ceiling by the light rays shining through the holes. I had to make sure that some of the holes in the can were much larger than others to show the varying brightness of stars in the constellations. The cans are stored in my portfolio file box along with a brief paragraph describing each one.

Reflection

I loved this activity because I could work with a friend, and we did it outside on the grass rather than indoors in the classroom. Sometimes it was hard to punch the nails through the lid and to make the stars different sizes. We used magic marker to outline the stars in each constellation before we punched the holes.

Two Reviews of

Picture Books about Outer Space

TITLE:

The Magic School Bus Lost in the Solar System

AUTHOR AND ILLUSTRATOR:

Joanna Cole

PUBLISHER:

Scholastic, 1990

The science books in the Magic School Bus series are excellent learning tools. They are colorful, interesting, and full of charts, graphs, pictures, and actual class notes.

The Magic School Bus Lost in the Solar System is about a group of students in Ms. Frizzle's class who take a field trip to the planetarium only to find it closed for repairs. All of a sudden, their bus turns into a spaceship and they are hurled into outer space. The children tour the skies and planets and even play on the moon.

When the children return to the classroom, they make a terrific chart and a solar system mobile. They warn other students not to attempt a space field trip because (1) attaching rockets to the school bus would upset your parents, (2) landing on some planets may be dangerous to your health, and (3) space travel could make you miss dinner with your family as well as the rest of your childhood.

My favorite parts of the book were the students' mini-reports on solar system topics. They were illustrated as if they were written on three-holed notebook paper and placed in the margins of the pages.

TITLE:

The Story of May

AUTHOR AND ILLUSTRATOR:

Mordicai Gerstein

PUBLISHER:

HarperCollins, 1993

This allegory of family love takes place throughout the seasons. Each month of the year has a special task to perform. Uncle October carves a pumpkin portrait, for example, while Cousin March brings May safely home to April, riding on the back of the early spring wind.

The main idea of the story is that the month of May, who lives with her mother, April, has never met her father, December. December lives in the bitter cold, far away across the year. During the warm spring months, May sets out to learn the secrets of her heritage. She gets lost and visits each month in an effort to find her father and then return to her home.

The illustrations in this book are colorful and beautiful. They almost tell the story by themselves.

Reflection

I enjoyed this activity very much. I have visual/spatial strength and picture books make it easy for me to read and learn. My audiotape turned out well and the first graders at the elementary school down the street liked it. They sent me a letter to thank me for giving the tape to them.

My ABC Fact Report:

The Solar System

PURPOSE

An ABC Fact Report is a list of 26 different solar system concepts, with each fact beginning with a letter of the alphabet. It is a basic summary of the important information about the topic, organized according to the alphabet.

WHAT I DID

I organized my notes from class readings, lectures, textbook assignments, discussions, and research according to the letters of the alphabet so that I could better remember the important ideas. Sometimes I didn't have a fact for one of the letters, so I had to find one.

My ABC Fact Report

Astronomy is the study of the universe and all of its stars, planets, asteroids, moons, and other objects.

Brightness of a star is called its magnitude or size. Big stars are brighter than little stars, and so have greater "absolute" magnitude. Stars close to Earth appear brighter than those further away and so have greater "apparent" magnitude.

Constellations are groups of stars related to each other according to how they appear to an observer on Earth.

Distances between objects in space are so great that astronomers do not use ordinary units of measurement like miles or kilometers, but use units such as a light-year (the distance light travels through space in one Earth year).

Ecliptic describes "the apparent path the sun and planets take across the sky."

First manned space flight took place in 1961 by the Russian Yuri Gagarin. First American in orbit was John Glenn in 1962.

Galaxy is a large group of stars. We live in the "Milky Way" galaxy.

H-R diagram is a chart that describes the colors of the stars and the amount of light each star emits.

Irregular galaxies are small groups of stars with no definite shape.

Jupiter is the largest planet of our solar system.

Kids have made heroes of astronauts like John Glenn, Neil Armstrong, David Scott, Frank Borman, and the first teacher in space, Christa McAuliffe.

Lunar phases refer to the different shapes of the moon, which depend upon where the moon is in its orbit.

Meteoroids are chunks or grains of rock traveling through space. When it enters Earth's atmosphere, a meteoroid is moving at about 45,000 miles per hour. As it plunges earthward, it heats up and disintegrates, leaving behind a "shooting star."

Neptune, Jupiter, Saturn, Uranus, and Pluto are called **outer planets** because they are very far from the sun.

Orbital velocity refers to the speed at which a planet travels along its orbit or path.

Pulsars are small stars that give off little light but send out radio waves.

Quasar refers to a large group of faraway stars that send out energy in the forms of radio waves and light.

Ring system refers to the bands of light around a planet. Saturn's rings are easily seen with a telescope.

Stars are formed when gravity pulls together clouds of gas and dust in deep space. As more gas and dust get pulled in, the clump heats up. Finally, heat and pressure make a fire called nuclear fusion.

Theory called the Big Bang Theory states that the universe was formed about 14 billion years ago in one giant explosion, called the "big bang."

Uranus is the seventh planet from the sun.

Venus, Mercury, Earth, and Mars are **inner planets.**

Weather forecasters use satellites to help them make predictions and understand weather conditions.

Xamples of the names of American spacecraft flown into space: Friendship 7, Gemini 8, and Apollo 10.

Years, days, and seasons are determined by the rotation of Earth around the sun.

Zest for knowledge can make one want to study the solar system.

Reflection

I found this activity very helpful at test time because it helped me organize my notes about the Solar System. I used the ABC facts to study for my test and to review the major ideas. Most of the students in my cooperative learning group had the same information as I did although there were some differences, too. It was hard to find facts for some of the letters, so we had to "fudge" a little on those.

My Portfolio Rubric/Conference Questions

RATING SCALE

1 = I could have done better.   2 = I did a good job.   3 = I did a terrific job.

ARTIFACTS

1. Organization and completeness of portfolio ☐1 ☐2 ☐3

2. Quality of artifacts selected ☐1 ☐2 ☐3

3. Creativity shown in work ☐1 ☐2 ☐3

4. Correctness of work (grammar, spelling, sentence structure, neatness, punctuation, etc.) ☐1 ☐2 ☐3

5. Evidence of learning concepts and/or applying skills ☐1 ☐2 ☐3

6. Reflection process ☐1 ☐2 ☐3

7. Evidence of enthusiasm and interest in assignments ☐1 ☐2 ☐3

8. Oral presentation of portfolio ☐1 ☐2 ☐3

QUESTIONS I WISH OTHERS WOULD ASK ME ABOUT MY PORTFOLIO

1. What was your favorite artifact and why?

2. What are the three most interesting things you learned during your study of the solar system and outer space?

3. What was your hardest task during this unit of study?

4. Would you ever want to be an astronaut, an astronomer, or a space scientist? Why?

5. Do you think the government should continue to spend so many tax dollars on space exploration? Give reasons for your answer.

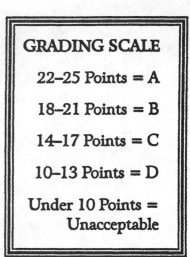

GRADING SCALE

22–25 Points = A

18–21 Points = B

14–17 Points = C

10–13 Points = D

Under 10 Points = Unacceptable

My Personal Comments

I really liked this unit because everything we did was fun and interesting. It was hard for me to decide which artifacts to include in this portfolio. My favorite activities were the creation of the charts, diagrams, and demonstrations, because I am good at visual/spatial tasks. The most difficult assignment was the ABC report because I am weakest in verbal/linguistic types of assignments.

A Very Practical Appendix

Student Activities to Integrate Instruction through Planning and Carrying out a Science Fair

1. Determine the main objectives of the science fair, and record them for class use.

2. Recruit volunteers (teachers and parents) who have good organizational skills and an interest in science to serve on the science fair committee.

3. Set a time, location, and date for the science fair.

4. Arrange for schedule, space, and total school involvement with the proper administrative staff.

5. Write the science fair rules. Include such things as the entry deadline, size limits for displays, requirements for final reports and logs of observations, the completion deadline, judging guidelines, and awards.

6. Compile a list of suggested science fair topics.

7. Design an entry form. Include a place for the student's name, project title, hypothesis, method, materials, and student and parent signatures.

8. Draft a cover letter (to be endorsed by the principal) which introduces the fair and explains the rules.

9. Design the evaluative criteria and a corresponding evaluation form. Include charts, graphs, and other appropriate measurement devices.

10. Publicize the application deadline, the date of the science fair, and the awards.

11. Prepare posters and bulletin board displays to be placed in the halls, the cafeteria, and in other common areas in order to generate interest throughout the school.

12. Contact and secure judges.

13. Plan the science fair layout. Draw a floor plan for efficiency.

14. Plan, type, and reproduce the science fair program.

15. Send each judge a judging packet which includes the fair rules, the judging criteria, and a list of the projects to be judged in his or her area of expertise. Arrange to meet with the entire judging panel if possible.

16. Order or make certificates, ranging from entry-level certificates to prize-level certificates, all explained in the evaluative criteria.

17. Gather the necessary materials and equipment such as tables, chairs, and a portable address system.

18. Send thank-yous to parent and teacher volunteers, judges, and demonstrators after the science fair.

Ten High-interest Strategies/Activities to Integrate Social Studies into Science

1 Study different types of maps and then create maps that depict the geographic features of different biomes, habitats of plants or animals, locations of important rock and mineral quarries, and home countries of famous scientists.

Example: Construct a map to show a worldwide location for each of the following biomes:

- grassland
- desert
- scrubland
- deciduous forest
- tundra
- coniferous forest
- tropical rain forest

2 Describe major scientific projects and programs and discuss their political and economic implications.

Example: Determine the political advantages and disadvantages that a presidential candidate would encounter if he or she supported increased funding for AIDS at the expense of funding for other health concerns and problems.

Example: Determine the political advantages and disadvantages of a Florida state senator's support of increased funding for the space program at the expense of funding for improving educational programs for a rapidly growing population.

3 Explore the societal values and ethics of important scientific research efforts.

Example: If you were going to establish rules and guidelines for awarding organ transplants to selected individuals, what criteria would you establish and what decision-making process would you use?

4 **Research the histories of the most significant natural disasters from around the world.**

Example: Determine the most devastating earthquake, tornado, hurricane, and volcano eruption ever to occur in recorded history.

5 **Study the ethnic and cultural backgrounds of various scientists.**

Example: Outline ten significant accomplishments of individual scientists. Determine the ethnic or cultural setting in which each scientist worked.

6 **Trace the historical development of major scientific theories, principles, discoveries, or breakthroughs.**

Example: Record the important events and experiences that led to the development of Newton's laws.

7 **Compare and contrast the operational definitions of related terms in social studies and science.**

Example: Compare and contrast the concept of "work" in a study of careers or occupations with that of "work" as related to energy and motion in the physical world of science.

8 **Use a "cause and effect" approach to analyze varied science-related topics and issues.**

Example: Determine the major causes and effects of efforts by conservationists to protect our national parks and forests.

9 **Relate the social science field of archaeology to the study of science topics and concepts.**

Example: Discuss the origins of fossils as they relate to the study of anthropology.

10 **Establish transportation and communication relationships that exist between the social studies and science areas.**

Example: Determine how the science of telecommunications has influenced the globalization of the world.

Ten High-interest Strategies/Activities to Integrate Math into Science

1 **Use Venn diagrams to show comparison and contrast.**

Example: Compare and contrast the planets Jupiter and Saturn, the Sun and the Moon, or comets and meteorites.

2 **Construct line, bar, circle, and pictographs.**

Example: Construct a line graph to show ten familiar animals of the world which are in danger of becoming less familiar because they have become endangered species.

3 **Create word or story problems.**

Example: Energy from food is measured in units called calories. Use a calorie counter or food chart to calculate the number of calories you have consumed for one entire day and one entire week. Teenage boys need about 2800 calories a day and girls the same age need about 2400 calories a day to stay healthy. Determine whether you met your ideal caloric intake each day and for a week.

4 **Use measurement and monetary systems of the United States and other countries.**

Example: Determine how much money is spent by the U.S. government on health care, space exploration, AIDS research, research for cancer and heart disease, and natural disaster assistance. Do the allocated dollars make sense in terms of human needs?

Example: Convert all measurements for an experiment that you have given in the English system to measurements of the metric system (or vice versa).

5 **Construct flow charts or diagrams to show processes for making or doing something.**

Example: Construct a diagram showing the major classification groups of three different animals according to kingdom, phylum, class, order, family, genus, and species.

6 **Discover the role and elements of geometry in different science content areas.**

Example: Determine the density and volume of different liquids using a variety of geometric shaped containers or find the density and volume of different metals using a variety of geometric shaped samples.

7 **Conduct individual or group surveys and show results in chart form.**

Example: Survey the students in your class to determine how many have inherited blue eyes, brown eyes, black eyes, and green eyes. Show your results in chart form.

8 **Use number codes or ancient number systems to rewrite science formulas or facts.**

Example: Use a number code to write three key facts about metamorphic rocks. See if a friend can decipher your code and uncover your facts.

9 **Construct timelines to establish the chronology of important events.**

Example: Make a timeline to show the most significant events in the area of space exploration over the last thirty years.

10 **Use such topics as optical illusions, symmetry, and proportions to explain scientific principles, theories, or concepts.**

Example: Research and cite as many examples as you can of symmetry in nature.

Ten High-interest Strategies/Activities to Integrate Language Arts into Science

1 **Write reports or speeches and give them orally.**

Example: Prepare a short "speech to inform" that answers a question like one of these: What is electricity? What is light? What is sound?

2 **Express information through various forms of poetry.**

Example: Describe a landform or a planet using these five poetry forms: haiku, diamante, free verse, concrete, and acrostic. Call your work: "Five Ways to Look at a Mountain" or "Five Ways to Look at Saturn."

3 **Use diaries or learning logs to record feelings, ideas, reflections, and observations.**

Example: After reading the biography of a famous scientist, create a series of diary events telling the reader more about his or her work and life.

4 **Use children's literature and picture books.**

Example: Collect a series of picture books about science topics. Write a synopsis of each book. Determine what makes these books appealing and informative. The "Magic Bus Series" is good for this purpose.

5 **Read folktales, legends, myths, and tall tales.**

Example: Select a favorite constellation to study and prepare a short picture essay that tells something about the story that inspired the naming of the constellation.

6 **Use the dictionary as a tool for acquiring information.**

Example: Use the dictionary to define these terms that are related to our study of light: lens, reflection, refraction, prism, and shadow.

7 **Write and send friendly or business letters.**

Example: Organize a letter campaign for the people in your school or community informing them of the dangers of toxic waste items such as pesticides, motor oils, paint solvents, and cleaning materials, and the rules for discarding them.

8 Write creative reports on science topics of your choice. Consider formats such as:

- ABC Reports
- Number Reports
- Puzzle Reports
- Comic Strip Reports
- Chalk Talk Reports

For details on these report formats, see *Making Portfolios, Products, and Performances Meaningful and Manageable for Students and Teachers* by Imogene Forte and Sandra Schurr, Incentive Publications, 1995.

Example: Write a Number Report about Mammals called "Ten Things Everyone Should Know About Mammals." Each paragraph is centered around one important point about mammals and contains a number or statistical piece of information. Be sure to include an opening or introductory paragraph and a closing or concluding paragraph.

9 Compose original short stories.

Example: Choose one of the following topics on which to write an original story related to our study of astronomy:

- The Martians Have Landed
- The Night I Spotted a UFO in Our Back Yard
- The Mysterious Planet X
- My First Flight in Space
- The Shooting Star That Got Lost

10 Incorporate grammar into tasks.

Example: Browse through your textbook (or a newspaper or news magazine) and select a picture depicting a science-related event or topic of special interest to you. Use it as a springboard for writing a declarative sentence, an interrogative sentence, an exclamatory sentence, and a sentence that gives a command, all related to the content of the picture.

Example: Make a list of common nouns, proper nouns, and verbs that best describe or explain:

- solids, liquids, and gases
- acids and bases
- chemical and physical changes
- mixtures and solutions
- elements of the periodic table

Topics for Student Reports

ASTRONOMY

The Earth-Moon System

The Solar System

Stars and Galaxies

The Sun

BIOLOGY

Basic Units of Life/Jobs of Cells

Breathing/Respiration

Circulation

Moving the Body (bones, muscles)

Nervous System

Reproduction/Heredity

BOTANY

How Plants Reproduce

Photosynthesis

CHEMISTRY

Chemical Reactions

Organic Chemistry

Periodic Table

ECOLOGY

Acid Rain

Changing Ecosystems

Environmental Issues and Conservation

Global Warming and the Greenhouse Effect

Pollution

GEOLOGY

Common Rocks

Earthquakes

Elements and Minerals

Energy Resources

Forces inside Earth

Geologic Time

Landforms

Natural Events that Shape the Land

Planet Earth

The Rock Cycle

Soil

Volcanoes

METEOROLOGY

Air

Atmospheric Pressure

Weather and Climate

OCEANOGRAPHY

Ocean Floor/Shore Zone

Water

PALEONTOLOGY

Dinosaurs

PHYSICS

Electricity and Magnetism

Electromagnetic Waves

Gases, Atoms, and Molecules

Heat and Temperature

Light

Machines

Motion

Moving Water

Sound

Structure of the Atom

Thermal Energy

Waves

Work and Energy

ZOOLOGY

Animal Communication

Animal Life

Differences between Warm-blooded and
   Cold-blooded Animals

How Animals Reproduce

Interactions in the Living World

The Invertebrates

The Vertebrates

Research Outline

Topic: _____

Key Questions

Resource Materials

Facts Discovered

Answers to Questions

Summary or Conclusion

NAME _____

DATE _____

Interdisciplinary Unit in Science

Title: _____

Topic (or Theme): _____

Purpose

Objectives

Glossary

Introductory Activity

Activities or Projects in Related Content Areas
Math

Social Studies

Language Arts

Enrichment or Exploratory

Homework or Independent Study Projects

Cooperative Learning Activity

Culminating Activity

Assessment

Integrating Science to Accommodate Multiple Intelligences

Science Theme: _____

	Social Studies	Math	Language Arts
VERBAL/ LINGUISTIC			
LOGICAL/ MATHEMATICAL			
VISUAL/SPATIAL			
BODY/ KINESTHETIC			
MUSICAL/ RHYTHMICAL			
INTERPERSONAL			
INTRAPERSONAL			

NOTE: Not every square need be filled in for every topic. Just make sure there is a good content balance in each unit.

Lesson Plan and Record Sheet for Developing an Integrated Approach to a Scientific Experiment Based on Bloom's Taxonomy

KNOWLEDGE
Materials needed: _____

_____

_____

COMPREHENSION
Outline for conducting the study:

_____

_____

_____

_____

APPLICATION
Chart for recording data observed and/or collected:

WHAT I DID	WHAT I OBSERVED

ANALYSIS
Conclusions drawn:

1. _____
2. _____
3. _____
4. _____

SYNTHESIS
Reflections on data to determine how different conclusions might have been drawn if variables were changed:

1. _____
2. _____
3. _____

EVALUATION
Degree of success as determined by set of group-generated criteria:

_____

_____

_____

_____

Integrating Science to Accommodate Williams' Taxonomy

Science Theme: _____

	Social Studies	Math	Language Arts
FLUENCY			
FLEXIBILITY			
ORIGINALITY			
ELABORATION			
RISK TAKING			
COMPLEXITY			
CURIOSITY			
IMAGINATION			

NOTE: Not every square need be filled in for every topic. Just make sure there is a good content balance in each unit.

Teacher Checklist to Aid in the Promotion of Journal Writing in the Science Classroom

Purposes

How do you present the purposes of a journal to your students when you are making journal assignments?

A journal is a . . .

a. _____ sourcebook/collection of ideas, thoughts, and opinions.

b. _____ place to write first drafts/outlines of papers and projects.

c. _____ place to record observations of and/or questions about something read, written, or discussed.

d. _____ recordkeeping tool to use to keep track of what and how much was read/researched on a topic.

e. _____ place in which to write personal reactions or responses to a textbook assignment, group discussion, research finding, or audiovisual resource.

f. _____ reference file to help a student monitor individual growth or progress in a given area.

g. _____ way for students to "dialogue" in written form with peers and teachers.

h. _____ place for a student to write about topics that he or she has chosen.

i. _____ place for reflections on and paraphrases of material learned.

Formats

Which of the following journal formats is most appealing to you?

a. _____ special notebooks

b. _____ segments of audiotapes

c. _____ file cards

d. _____ handmade diaries

Writing Time

Which of the following time options is most practical for you?

a. _____ daily for five minutes

b. _____ semi-weekly for ten minutes

c. _____ weekly for fifteen minutes

d. _____ when needed

Student Feedback

Which of these formal/informal methods makes most sense to you?

a. _____ student sharing of journal entries with peers

b. _____ reading journal entries aloud to class on a volunteer basis

c. _____ using journals for "conferencing"

d. _____ taking journal entries home to share with parents/guardians

e. _____ analyzing and answering one's own journal entry one or more days after entry was recorded to acknowledge personal changes in perspective

Annotated Bibliography

An annotated bibliography of Incentive Publications titles selected to provide additional help for integrating instruction in science

Breeden, Terri. *Cooperative Learning Companion.* Nashville, TN: Incentive Publications, 1992. *(Grades 5–8)*
A winning collection of creative teaching aids, including reproducible charts, forms, and posters, along with comprehensive instructions for setting up a smoothly-running and effective cooperative classroom environment.

Breeden, Terri and Emalie Egan. *Strategies and Activities to Raise Achievement.* Nashville, TN: Incentive Publications, 1995. *(Grades 4–8)*
Comprehensive manual contains high-interest activities and esteem-building exercises that will motivate students to become more effective test-takers and lifelong learners.

Forte, Imogene and Sandra Schurr. *The Cooperative Learning Guide and Planning Pak for Middle Grades.* Nashville, TN: Incentive Publications, 1992. *(Grades 5–8)*
A collection of high-interest thematic units, thematic thinking skills projects, and thematic poster projects. Includes reference skills sharpeners and much more.

—. *The Definitive Middle School Guide: A Handbook for Success.* Nashville, TN: Incentive Publications, 1993. *(Grades 5–8)*
This comprehensive, research-based manual provides the perfect overview for educators and administrators who are determined to establish a school environment that stimulates and motivates the Middle Grade student in the learning process.

—. *Interdisciplinary Units and Projects for Thematic Instruction for Middle Grade Success.* Nashville, TN: Incentive Publications, 1994. *(Grades 5–8)*
A jumbo-sized collection of thematic-based interdisciplinary activities and assignments that was created to spark interest, encourage communication, and promote problem solving as well as decision making.

—. *Making Portfolios, Products, and Performances Meaningful and Manageable for Students and Teachers.* Nashville, TN: Incentive Publications, 1995. *(Grades 4–8)*
Filled with valuable information and specific suggestions for incorporating authentic assessment techniques that help students enjoy a more active role in the evaluation process. Includes a convenient pull-out Graphic Organizer with creative ideas for integrating content instruction and appraising student understanding.

—. *Middle Grades Advisee/Advisor Program.* Nashville, TN: Incentive Publications, 1991. *(Grades 5–8)*
A comprehensive program dedicated to meeting the needs and confronting the challenges of today's young adolescent students. A flexible, manageable curriculum, available at three different levels, that contains both a teacher's guide and over 300 reproducible activities on essential topics.

—. *Science Mind Stretchers*. Nashville, TN: Incentive Publications, 1987. *(Grades 4–7)*
This complete handbook uses a thematic mini-unit format to explore basic science concepts, motivate use of vital reasoning skills, and encourage understanding and use of science process skills.

—. *Tools, Treasures, and Measures for Middle Grade Success*. Nashville, TN: Incentive Publications, 1994. *(Grades 5–8)*
This practical resource offers a wide assortment of teaching essentials, from ready-to-use lesson plans and student assignments to valuable lists and assessment tools.

Frender, Gloria. *Learning to Learn*. Nashville, TN: Incentive Publications, 1990. *(All grades)*
This comprehensive reference book is filled with creative ideas, practical suggestions, and "hands on" materials to help students acquire the organizational, study, test-taking, and problem-solving skills they need to become lifelong effective learners.

—. *Teaching for Learning Success: Practical Strategies and Materials for Everyday Use*. Nashville, TN: Incentive Publications, 1994. *(All grades)*
This ready-to-use resource has the materials needed to successfully implement cooperative learning techniques, organize and manage the classroom environment, adapt teaching to suit varied learning styles, and promote the home-school connection.

Graham, Leland and Darriel Ledbetter. *How to Write a Great Research Paper*. Nashville, TN: Incentive Publications, 1994. *(Grades 5–8)*
Simplify the research process with these mini-lessons. Help students choose and narrow topics, locate appropriate information from a variety of sources, take notes, organize an outline, develop a rough draft, document sources, as well as write, revise, and evaluate their final papers.

Opie, Brenda and Lori Jackson and Douglas McAvinn. *Masterminds Decimals, Percentages, Metric System, and Consumer Math*. Nashville, TN: Incentive Publications, 1995. *(Grades 4–8)*
These high-interest student activities, designed for today's middle grades science programs, are based on measurement instruction using metric units and decimal values.

Science YELLOW PAGES for Students and Teachers. Nashville, TN: Incentive Publications, 1988. *(Grades 2–8)*
A virtual "treasure chest" containing valuable facts, lists, charts, and definitions related to science laws and principles, formulas, experiments, investigations, and more.

Spivack, Doris and Geri Blond. *Inventions and Extensions*. Nashville, TN: Incentive Publications, 1991. *(Grades 3–7)*
A unique resource containing activities based on information about famous inventors and their inventions; designed to expand kids' natural curiosity about how things work, and to stimulate use of critical thinking and problem-solving skills.

Index

Index entries in bold type are titles of student activities.